Dictionary of Cognitive Psychology

of related interest

Dictionary of Developmental Psychology
Ian Stuart-Hamilton
ISBN 1 85302 200 4

Dictionary of Psychological Testing, Assessment and Treatment
Ian Stuart-Hamilton
ISBN 1 85302 201 2

Dictionary of Cognitive Psychology

Ian Stuart-Hamilton

Jessica Kingsley Publishers
London and Bristol, Pennsylvania

First published in the United Kingdom in 1995 by
Jessica Kingsley Publishers Ltd
116 Pentonville Road
London N1 9JB, England
and
1900 Frost Road, Suite 101
Bristol, PA 19007, U S A

Copyright © 1995 Ian Stuart-Hamilton

Library of Congress Cataloging in Publication Data
Stuart-Hamilton, Ian.
Dictionary of cognitive psychology / Ian Stuart-Hamilton.
p.   cm.
ISBN 1-85302-202-0
1. Cognitive psychology--dictionaries. 2. Cognitive psychology--Miscellanea. I. Title.
BF201.S78   1995
153'.03--dc20   95-6413
                                                               CIP

British Library Cataloguing in Publication Data
Stuart-Hamilton, Ian
Dictionary of Cognitive Psychology
I. Title
153.4

ISBN 1 85302 202 0

Printed and Bound in Great Britain by
Athenaeum Press, Gateshead, Tyne and Wear

To Messrs Holmes and Kimber
Signum scientis est posse docere.

Acknowledgements

My usual, but no less profuse, thanks to my wife for reading and editing the manuscript – a deed of heroic proportions. My fulsome gratitude also to Elizabeth Maylor, who read the penultimate draft of this book, and made a number of extremely useful suggestions. My thanks to Rosie Barker and Jessica Kingsley.

Introduction

This dictionary provides descriptions of the main terms found in cognition. The aim is to provide the reader with a quick guide to the key concepts and terminology employed in the subject. Given the (inexplicable) fondness many cognitive psychologists display for neologisms, many of which last for only a journal article or two, only terms which have entered into general currency are included. However, terms which are not derived from cognition, but which are frequently cited in some branches of the subject (e.g. certain neurological and linguistic terms) *are* included.

Despite our most earnest efforts, there will be terms which I (and my editors and advisors) have missed, and researchers I have (unwittingly) slighted by not giving their work the same prominence as others'. I therefore issue the traditional request of compilers, that readers inform me of missing entries so that they can be considered fot insertion in any future edition of this dictionary.

Dr Ian Stuart-Hamilton
Principal Lecturer in Psychology,
Worcester College of Higher Education

Guide to use

Cross-references are in italics. Four caveats are required, arising from a desire to avoid unnecessary repetition or superfluous entries and definitions.

(1) Very occasionally, italicized words' entries are in a slightly different grammatical form (e.g. *samples* may actually be entered as **sample**).

(2) Within a definition, an italicized word in bold type (e.g. ***definition*** rather than *definition*) indicates that the term is fully defined within the entry being read. The word's own entry will simply refer the reader back to this definition.

(3) An entry followed only by a word or phrase in italics indicates a synonym, which should be consulted for the full definition.

(4) Words linked by a hyphen are treated as if there is a space between them.

There are relatively few inverted headings – entries are usually given the word order they have in normal text. Therefore, if the reader looks up 'semantic memory', he or she finds **semantic memory**, not an irritating note to see **memory, semantic.** If the reader should be aware of related terms, then a cross-reference is provided. Where an inverted heading has been used, it is for clear logical reasons.

There are entries for some key studies and experiments. Where a date is provided, this is so that the reader can gauge the age of the theory being discussed; it provides a check that the dictionary is referring to the same study he or she is reading about. There is no bibliography, since this book is intended as a quick guide, not a textbook manqué.

A

a posteriori That which can only be deduced from observation of the outside world. This contrasts with a *priori*, which is that which can be deduced without reference to the outside world.

a priori See *a posteriori*.

a priori plausibility *principle of a priori plausibility.*

AB design Shorthand for the stages in an experimental design. 'AB' denotes that there are two separate phases. The shorthand can of course be applied to other designs, e.g. 'ABA' indicates that the first stage is repeated after a second, different section, 'ABC' indicates three separate stages, etc.

ability test The term is a confusing one – some researchers use it synonymously with *achievement test*, others with *aptitude test*. Since the everyday use of the word 'ability' is similarly ambiguous, it is a term best avoided.

absolute error See *true scores theory*.

absolute knowledge Knowledge of facts which are absolute and unwavering (e.g. the Battle of Waterloo took place in 1815, the sun is a star, etc.).

absolute rating Rating made without comparison with other stimuli.

absolute sensitivity *absolute threshold.*

absolute threshold See *threshold*.

abstract identification Identifying an item by its status rather than its physical appearance.

abstract intelligence (1) The ability to process abstract concepts. This is contrasted with *concrete intelligence* – the

ability to deal with practical problems and 'real life' situations. (2) In some theories of psychological development, particularly those of, or influenced by, Jean Piaget, the term 'abstract intelligence' has much the same meaning as above. However, 'concrete intelligence' means a rather inferior method of thinking, in which the subject (an as yet undeveloped young child) is restricted to only being able to think about what s/he can see – genuine abstraction of thought is held to be beyond him/her.

abstract rule theory Any theory which proposes that problem-solving or other logical processes take place at an abstract, symbolic level.

abstraction The process of creating an abstract principle (usually describing a set of physical data).

absurdity test Test (usually of intelligence) in which the subject must identify what is wrong with an illogical statement or picture.

acalculia An inability to perform basic arithmetic skills, resulting from brain damage.

access code In many *mental models*, the format in which an item must be presented for it to be processed by a particular stage in the model.

accessible memory A memory which can be retrieved without *cues*. This contrasts with *available memories*, which are all those memories which can be retrieved immediately, plus those which are only retrievable after the use of cues or other prompts.

accretion Adding a considerable quantity of new information to an existing *schema*, without altering its basic structure. Compare with *restructuring* and *tuning*.

accuracy test Any test in which the accuracy of the answers, rather than time taken to answer, is of prime importance.

achievement test A measure of what the subject is currently capable of (e.g. a child's scholastic attainment). Compare with *aptitude test*.

acoustic code Mental representation of acoustic material.

acoustic coding *Encoding* a word or letter in terms of how it sounds.

acoustic confusion (1) Falsely perceiving/remembering a word or letter which sounds similar to the true word/letter. (2) Sometimes used as a synonym of the *acoustic similarity effect*.

acoustic cue A *cue* which prompts recall by drawing attention to an acoustic feature of the to-be-remembered item.

acoustic feature (1) A feature of an item which has acoustic properties. (2) The physical properties of a sound (e.g. its wavelength).

acoustic similarity effect (1) The phenomenon whereby a list of similar-sounding items (words, letters, etc.) is harder to remember than a list of dissimilar-sounding items. (2) Sometimes used as a synonym for *acoustic confusion*.

acquired aphasia See *aphasia*.

acquired dissimilarity *acquired distinctiveness*.

acquired distinctiveness Learning to distinguish between items which were initially perceived as identical. A yearly task of teachers and lecturers. See *acquired similarity*.

acquired dysgraphia A profound difficulty in spelling/writing resulting from brain damage.

acquired dyslexia A profound difficulty in reading resulting from brain damage. This takes various forms, some of which resemble *developmental dyslexics* or children learning to read (see *phonological dyslexia* and *surface dyslexia*), and one form (*demented dyslexia*) is usually associated with dementia. See *attentional dyslexia, deep dyslexia, direct dyslexia, letter-by-letter reading, phonological dyslexia, surface dyslexia* and contrast with *alexia*.

acquired similarity The (mis)perception of dissimilar items as identical, because the subject has learnt to place them in the same category. See *acquired distinctiveness*.

acquisition process An *input process* concerned with acquiring information and converting it for storage in memory.

acronym technique Method of *reduction coding* in which the to-be-remembered information is encoded as an acronym, which is more easily remembered, and which acts as a prompt.

ACT *adaptive control of thought*.

ACT* Acronym given to the latest (at time of writing) version of the *adaptive control of thought* model.

act psychology School of psychological thought active in the late nineteenth century, which concentrated on the totality of the mental experience and the act of thinking, rather than on the sub-processes of thought.

action schema A *schema* comprised of a collection or sequence of actions necessary to accomplish a particular task. A failure in this process can result in a *slip of action*.

action slip *slip of action.*

activation (1) The degree to which a memory is currently available for conscious inspection (i.e whether we are thinking about something). (2) The level of activity within a particular *node*. (3) Generally, the level of activity (often with the consideration of how close to *threshold* this is).

activation density (parallel distributed processing) The proportion of a *neural network* which is active at any one time. Generally, the lower the density, the more efficient the performance.

activation level See *level of activation.*

activation, level of *level of activation.*

activation-verification (AV) model Model of reading process (particularly pronouncing words) devised by Paap *et al.*

active list The set of *nodes* active at any one time in a system.

active memory (1) *short-term memory* (particularly *working memory*). (2) Memory for items and events where a conscious effort has been made to remember them. See *passive memory.*

active rehearsal *active memory*, definition (2)

active vocabulary The vocabulary a person uses when speaking or writing. This is usually smaller in size than his/her *passive vocabulary*, which is the total number of words s/he can understand when listening or reading.

ad hoc category A grouping of items which is created for a particular 'one off' situation, with the understanding that the items would never normally be grouped together.

adaptive control of thought (ACT) *Mental model* by Anderson of thought and memory. Inter alia, argues that *LTM* is composed of *declarative knowledge/memory* and *procedural knowledge/memory*. The latter are composed of *productions*, which are sets of 'If x occurs then do y' type rules. Anderson argues that people begin by learning declarative knowledge, before progressing to simple productions, which become more complex the more expert the person becomes. See also *strengthening* and *composition.*

adaptive control theory *adaptive control of thought.*

addition solution See *water jar problem.*

additive bilingualism Acquisition of a second language, with the first continuing to be used. This contrasts with **subtractive bilingualism,** in which the second language supplants the first.

additive factor modelling A method of assessing whether two or more factors are affecting the same stage in a process, by seeing if they statistically interact on the said stage.

additive stages process A process in which each or some of its sub-stages build upon the work performed by the previous sub-stages.

addressed phonology See *addressed pronunciation.*

addressed pronunciation The pronunciation of a word which is performed by consulting a memory of how to pronounce the word in question (the **addressed phonology**). This contrasts with **assembled pronunciation**, in which the word's pronunciation is built up from knowledge of how particular letters and letter sequences are usually pronounced (the **assembled phonology**). The latter option is the only one available for pronouncing unknown words, whilst the former may be used to pronounce familiar words (particularly those with *irregular spellings*). See *pronunciation by analogy*.

ADL *assessment of daily living*.

adversarial problem Problem in which not only ones own actions but also those of an opponent must be considered (e.g. a chess problem). By extension, a *non-adversarial problem* is one in which there is no opponent to be considered.

AFC *alternative forced choice task*.

AFF *auditory flutter fusion*.

affect emotion.

affirmation of the consequent In *conditional reasoning*, erroneously concluding that the *antecedent* must be true because the *consequent* is. See *denial of the antecedent*.

affirming the consequent *affirmation of the consequent*.

affordances See *Gibson's theory of direct perception*.

age norm The mean score for a given age group, and hence the score one would expect an average person of that age group to possess.

age of acquisition (AOA) The age at which a particular skill or piece of knowledge (e.g. how to read a particular word) was acquired.

agent (linguistics) The person performing the action described.

agentive case See *case grammar*.

agnosia A profound failure of recognition. A suffix indicates that the agnosia is in one particular sense – e.g. 'visual agnosia' is the inability to recognize objects by sight.

AH intelligence tests A collection of *fluid intelligence* tests (ranging in difficulty from '1', the easiest, to '6', the hardest) devised by Alice Heim (hence the name). Each test is generally in two sub-sections. The first assesses numerical and verbal logical reasoning, whilst the second assesses *visuo-spatial* skills.

AI *artificial intelligence*.

aided recall *cued recall*.

Aitken, Professor *Professor Aitken*.

alertness The hypothesized amount of a subject's *mental capacity* which is primed and ready for immediate use (the greater the amount primed, the higher the level of alertness).

alexia A complete failure to read or to recognize words or letters (in *dyslexia* there is a partial ability). Only usually seen in brain-damaged individuals.

alexia without agraphia *letter-by-letter reading*.

algorithm A problem-solving method which, appropriately applied, will inevitably yield the correct solution. See *heuristic*.

alignment heuristic Phenomenon whereby people tend to treat visual items which are not aligned on a common axis as if they are. This makes processing/memorization easier, if less accurate.

allocation In theories which assume a limited *mental capacity*, the apportioning of capacity to different processes which need to be simultaneously run.

allomorph Different letter combinations or sounds signifying the same meaning. E.g. the 'i' in 'stimuli' and 'es' in 'foxes' both denote the plural form. See *morpheme*.

allophone See *phone*.

alternating case See *case (letters)*.

alternative forced choice task (AFC) See *recognition task*.

A.M. Pseudonym of the patient whose symptoms and behaviour were reported in an often-cited case study of *phonological dyslexia*.

amnesia A failure of memory, usually abnormally severe, arising from e.g. stroke, head injury, illness, or poisoning. The term is occasionally used for memory loss which is usual or not unduly serious in its effects (e.g. *childhood amnesia*). *Anterograde amnesia* is amnesia for events which took place after the brain damage occurred (see *amnestic syndrome*). *Retrograde amnesia* is amnesia for events preceding the brain damage (usually this is confined to memory failure for a brief period before the damage occurred, rather than the patient's entire past life). *Source amnesia* refers to an inability to recognize where, when and how one learnt a piece of information, as opposed to the accuracy of recall of the information itself. 'Amnesia', strictly speaking, means total memory loss, though it is rarely used as such: most patients have some vestige of *mnemonic* skill. See *post-traumatic amnesia*.

amnesic aphasia *anomic aphasia.*

amnesic syndrome *amnestic syndrome.*

amnestic dysgraphia Severe form of *dysgraphia* in which the patient, although able to form individual letters, has the key symptoms of both *phonological dysgraphia* and *surface dysgraphia.*

amnestic syndrome *Amnesia* resulting from brain damage (either injury or damage from toxins, alcohol, etc.) where there are no other severe intellectual impairments. Some commentators treat the syndrome as synonymous with *anterograde amnesia*, although others include *retrograde amnesia* as well.

analog representation *analogue representation.*

analogical inference *Inference* that an event is similar to one encountered before, and can be dealt with in an analogous manner.

analogical mapping The process of recognizing an analogy between items or events.

analogical problem solving *analogical inference.*

analogical reasoning Reasoning in which an answer is sought by considering another problem with a similar structure whose solution is already known.

analogue code *analogue representation.*

analogue representation The representation of an item or event by a representation of its dimensions and appearance. E.g. a mental analogue representation of a line of animals going into Noah's Ark might be a 'mental picture' of a row of animals. In contrast, a *propositional representation* is a representation of an item or event in symbolic form. E.g. the animals might be represented by a list, with no accompanying visual imagery – 'two aardvarks, two aardwolfs, two anteaters' etc. A key division between the two modes of representation is that the analogue representation attempts to show the physical features of the items, whilst the propositional representation does not.

analogy, problem solving by *analogical inference.*

analogy, pronunciation by See *pronunciation by analogy.*

analogy test Problem-solving test in which subjects must identify the logic of an analogy in an example, and then provide a similar analogy (usually from a multiple choice). E.g. 'kippers are to marmalade as soup is to: (a) washing powder (b) mashed potatoes (c) hot chocolate (d) penguins'.

analysis by synthesis *Top-down processing*, often with the additional consideration that information from *bottom-up processing* shapes the procedure.

analysis by synthesis perception *cyclic model of perception*.

analytic statement A statement which is true by definition (e.g. 'God is omnipotent').

anaphora *anaphoric reference*.

anaphoric reference Referring to a previously named person, persons, thing or things by the appropriate pronoun (e.g. mentioning 'Michael' and then citing the same character as 'he'). I.e. using an *antecedent*.

anchor and adjust heuristic *Heuristic* in which the subject begins by making a general estimate and then 'fine tunes' it in the light of further information.

anchor point A point of reference on a scale against which a subject makes his/her judgements.

animal cognition The study of cognitive processes in non-human animals.

annealing (parallel distributed processing) The final resting state of a *neural network* when the pattern of excitation has been 'calculated'.

anoetic See *noetic*.

anomia Inability to name. The term is usually reserved for severe cases resulting from brain damage.

anomic aphasia *Aphasia* characterized by an inability to find specific words. The term is largely interchangeable with *anomia*.

answer until correct (AUC) score Marking system for a multiple choice test, in which a subject makes as many attempts as necessary until s/he obtains

the right answer; the more attempts made, the fewer points scored. See *inferred number right (INR) score*.

antecedent (1) See *conditional reasoning*. (2) In linguistics, a reference to an earlier item in a communication.

anterograde amnesia See *amnesia*.

antonym test Test in which the subject must supply the opposite of a word supplied by the experimenter.

AOA *age of acquisition*.

aphasia Failure of language. Strictly speaking, the term refers to an entire loss of language (a partial failure is *dysphasia*), but it is generally used for any language failure. Also, it usually refers to *acquired aphasia* – i.e. the patient has acquired it through accident or illness, and prior to this s/he had usual linguistic abilities. Aphasia can be broadly divided into three categories – *receptive aphasia* is a specific failure to understand language, *expressive aphasia* a failure to produce it, and *global aphasia* a failure of both comprehension and production. For more specific categories, see *anomic aphasia, ataxic aphasia, audio-verbal aphasia, auditory aphasia, Broca's aphasia, conduction aphasia, developmental aphasia, mixed transcortical aphasia, transcortical aphasia, transcortical motor aphasia, transcortical sensory aphasia,* and *Wernicke's aphasia*. See also *jargon aphasia*.

apprehension span *span of apprehension*.

approximate visual access Misreading a word as one which looks similar (e.g. 'house' for 'horse').

approximation to English Technique used to create 'sentences' whose resemblance to grammatical and meaningful prose can be systematically varied. At its most garbled, words are chosen at random from the dictionary. To produce more meaningful levels, subjects are given a 'Chinese whispers' type game in which they add words on to those provided by other subjects. The more words they are allowed to add, and the more they are allowed to see of what previous subjects wrote, the more meaningful the resulting prose. The sentences are used in e.g. prose memory experiments.

aptitude test A measure of what the subject is potentially capable of, even though s/he may not currently attain such heights (e.g. an *IQ* test might show that a child's teaching is not stretching him/her sufficiently). Compare with *achievement test*.

architecture *cognitive architecture.*

archival memory The memories of everything a subject learns.

armchair experiment *gedanken experiment.*

arousal The general level of activation in the body and/or mind.

arrangement problem Type of measure of problem-solving ability in which the subject must rearrange elements in an array to arrive at the correct answer (e.g. conundrums).

articulatory coding *Encoding* an item (word, letter, etc.) in terms of how it is articulated (i.e. the mechanisms used in pronouncing its name).

articulatory level *phonetic level.*

articulatory loop Term for a component in the original *working memory* model. The term has been superseded by *phonological loop*. This is because the loop was initially presumed to rely on *articulatory coding*, but later evidence pointed towards a *phonological coding* mechanism.

articulatory modality Pertaining to any stimuli which can be spoken.

articulatory representation A mental image stored as what is subjectively perceived as words being spoken 'silently' (i.e. there are muscular movements associated with speaking the words, but they are not powerful enough, nor is breath exhaled, so the sounds are not heard). Compare with *auditory representation*. Words represented in this manner are said to use a **speech code**.

articulatory store *articulatory loop.*

articulatory suppression *concurrent articulation.*

artifact An incidental by-product of an experimental method, which may colour the results.

artificial category A category whose membership rules have been created by a human or artificial intelligence programme according to a set of specific rules. These rules are usually more exacting than those of a *natural category* (e.g. a tomato may be classified as a vegetable in a natural category, but an artificial category might, more logically, designate it as a fruit).

artificial intelligence (AI) (1) Any method of performing (and usually with the implication of impersonating) an aspect of intellectual (or more generally, psychological) functioning using computer programming. (2) The study of the same. Either definition may be concerned with improving knowledge of how the human mind performs, and/or in producing a better computer programme. Note that the programmes do not necessarily have to mimic human performance, nor test a model of human thought processes. If these goals are specifically sought, then the procedure can be classified as *computer simulation (CS)*. If they are not, then the term *machine intelligence* is often used.

ascender In *lower case* letters, a segment of a letter which rises above the height of the main 'body'. E.g. 'k' and 't' have ascenders, whilst 'a' and 'o' do not. By the same token, *descender* refers to a segment of a letter which falls below the line of text (e.g. 'p' and 'q' have descenders, 'k' and 'a' do not). The presence of ascenders and descenders may be important in word and letter recognition.

assembled phonology See *addressed pronunciation*.

assembled pronunciation See *addressed pronunciation*.

assessment of daily living (ADL) A n y method of measuring daily activities, usually with the purpose of identifying memory slips, etc.

assimilation (1) In recalling a story, lengthy piece of prose, etc., altering the plot/other information to conform more closely to prior knowledge, vocabulary, etc. (2) In developmental psychology (particularly the work of or following Piaget), the term usually denotes an attempt to understand an event/item/person using an existing *schema*, and is contrasted with 'accommodation', which is the integration of new information into an existing schema.

association A perceived link between two or more items or events (usually learnt). The term is used in e.g. memory experiments to denote how intrinsically connected the to-be-remembered items are. Items with strong links (e.g. 'bread' and 'butter') have a *high association*, whilst weakly linked items (e.g. 'dog' and 'lamp') have a *low association*.

association cortex See *primary cortex*.

association time The time taken to produce an association (e.g. of meaning or of similar sound) to a given item.

association value The degree to which subjects can ascribe meaning to a supposedly meaningless stimulus (e.g. a *nonsense word*).

associational fluency Fluency in producing similes or synonyms. Often tested by giving a subject a list of words and asking for their synonyms.

associationist theory of memory T h e theory, first proposed by Ebbinghaus in the late nineteenth century, which states that items which are encountered at the same time tend to be associated with each other and remembered as a cluster. The process was felt to be passive. The theory has been largely refuted, although the basic experimental findings by Ebbinghaus on, inter alia, the rate of forgetting, are still recognized as valid.

associative activation *Slip of action* in which the subject begins an erroneous sequence of actions because they are strongly associated with the actions s/he was supposed to perform.

associative inhibition The degree to which the memory for one item is interfered with by memory for another item (e.g. *proactive inhibition* and *retroactive inhibition*).

associative interference *associative inhibition*.

associative learning Learning the association between items and/or events. Hence, by extension, learning to predict an item or event given another item/event with which it has previously been associated.

associative meaning The thoughts generated upon encountering a particular word.

associative memory Memory for a link between items.

associative net (1) *associative network*. (2) Particular type of *associative network* in which the connections between *nodes* and inputs and outputs can be altered by *Hebbian rules*.

associative network A structure in which changes in one component may influence other components. The term is applied to the structure of many *mental models*.

associative priming *semantic facilitation*.

associative stage (skill acquisition) See *cognitive stage (skill acquisition)*.

associative store *content addressable memory*.

associative strength The 'strength' of the connection between items in a mental store. Generally, this refers to the ease with which one of these items can activate (e.g. in *semantic facilitation*).

ataxic aphasia *Aphasia* due to an an inability to articulate.

Atkinson-Shiffrin memory model *modal memory model*.

atmosphere hypothesis Theory that subjects make certain types of errors in *syllogisms* because the concluding statement (whose validity the subject must judge) is written in the same terms as the preceding statements. E.g. errors will be higher when judging the validity of 'if A then B, if B then C, if A then C' than in judging 'if A then B, if B then C, if A then not C'.

ATN *augmented transition network*.

ATRANS See *primitive action*.

attended message The information which is attended to in a *selective attention* task.

attention The ability to concentrate on a *target* item(s) or task at hand despite distracting stimuli. See *distractibility, divided attention, focused attention, selective attention,* and *sustained attention*.

attention span (1) *span of apprehension*. (2) The length of time a subject can attend to the same stimulus.

attention spotlight A model of *attention* by Posner which conceptually presents attention as a spotlight which focuses on the information which is its subject. When attention has to be shifted to another item, expanded, narrowed, etc., this is viewed in terms of the spotlight having to be moved into a new position, re-focused, etc., and the time taken to do this (and the possible errors it may create) are seen as analogous to the attentional process. See *microspotlight*.

attentional blob The finite quantity of *attention* which a person has at their disposal – the blob can be concentrated on one task, or spread more thinly over several.

attentional dyslexia An *acquired dyslexia* in which the patient reads segments of separate words as a whole (e.g. 'kill' and 'sock' read as 'kick'). See *migration error*.

attentional process (1) *Processing stage* responsible for attending to the item or event which is to be processed, to the exclusion of distractions. (2) The execution of a task which requires conscious control for its successful completion. Contrast with *automatic process*.

attentional selectivity The degree to which a subject can concentrate specifically on the item or event to which s/he is supposed to attend.

attentional width *width of attention.*

attentive process *attentional process.*

attenuated filter See *attenuation theory.*

attenuation theory Theory of *selective attention* which argues that *unattended messages* are processed, but not to the same depth as the *attended message.* The mechanism by which this is done is called the *attenuated filter.* This is in contrast to some more basic forms of the *bottleneck theories*, which argue that the unattended messages are ignored completely.

attribute identification I d e n t i f y i n g those features of an item/situation which are necessary to identify the whole correctly.

attribute model *set-theoretic model.*

attributes In a *schema* theory, the typical features of an item/situation which one would expect to be present (e.g. a dog schema might include attributes of fur, tail, etc.). However, the attributes can usually take several forms (e.g. long fur, short fur, long tail, short tail, etc.), called *values.*

AUC score *answer until correct score.*

audience design The degree to which a message is tailored to suit the comprehension of a particular recipient.

audio-verbal aphasia An inability to comprehend phrases (although comprehension of single words may be intact).

auditory agnosia An inability to recognize an item, event, etc., by its sound.

auditory analysis system Name given to a variety of models of how the mind processes auditory information. Typically, the emphasis is on how *phonological* information is processed.

auditory aphasia An inability to comprehend spoken language.

auditory cortex Collective term for areas of the *cortex* responsible for collating and interpreting auditory information. Principally located in the *temporal lobe* (see *primary auditory cortex*).

auditory flutter fusion (AFF) The rate at which a pulsing sound must repeat itself for it to be heard as a continuous sound.

auditory lexicon Hypothesized mental store of sounds (particularly word sounds), which enable the subject to recognize items as having been encountered before. Note that usually the model does not suppose that the lexicon recognizes the meaning of the item. In most models this is the task of the *semantic system.*

auditory masking See *masking.*

auditory modality Pertaining to any stimuli which can be heard.

auditory representation A mental image stored in what is subjectively perceived as a 'sound' or 'voice' in the head. Compare with *articulatory representation.*

auditory sensory memory *echoic memory.*

auditory suffix effect The phenomenon whereby any speech sound presented after a list of to-be-remembered items will impair memory for the list, though non-speech sounds will usually not have an effect.

auditory type Subject whose *mental imagery* is primarily auditory. The phrase is sometimes applied to readers who have a tendency to read words by mentally 'sounding them out'. This contrasts with the *visual type*, whose imagery (and reading) is predominantly visual.

augmented transition network (ATN) *Transition network* model. The 'augmented' prefix refers to the fact that the model uses memory stores to aid interpretation (e.g. memorizing the nouns can help in interpreting *anaphoric references*).

Austin See *Lana.*

auto-association (parallel distributed processing) Model of mental functioning in which items are represented as different patterns on a *neural net.* The *weights* of the interconnections can be altered (typically, using *Hebbian rules*), thereby enabling the network to represent new items, to create more accurate representations, etc.

autobiographical memory Memory for events which are specific to an individual person's life, rather than a shared experience with others of the same general background and age.

automatic process The execution of a task which requires no conscious control for its successful completion. In a *partially automatic process*, the subject has some conscious awareness of the process, which is largely controlled by *contention scheduling.* See *controlled process* and contrast with *attentional process.*

automaticity The degree to which a process is an *automatic process.*

autonoetic See *noetic.*

autonomous stage (skill acquisition) See *cognitive stage (skill acquisition).*

AV model *activation-verification model.*

availability heuristic The *heuristic* whereby the more one can imagine about something, the more likely one is to believe in its existence.

available memory See *accessible memory.*

B

back propagation algorithm *backward propagation.*

BackProp *backward propagation.*

backpropagation *backward propagation.*

backpropagation of the Delta rule *backward propagation.*

backward association Learning a connection with an event which occurred earlier.

backward error propagation *backward propagation.*

backward masking See *masking.*

backward memory search In searching through one's (usually *autobiographical*) memories, starting with the memories of recent events and searching chronologically backwards. Compare with *forward memory search.*

backward propagation Concept employed in some models of *parallel distributed processing.* The obvious goal of any system is that its output should accurately represent the input. Backward propagation accomplishes this by means of trial and error learning. After the model has made a first attempt at producing the desired output, the output is compared with the input, and the nature of the discrepancy noted. Backward propagation adjusts the layer of *hidden units* immediately before the output, so that their pattern of excitation more closely matches that of the input. Hidden units on the next layer are then adjusted, and so on, with each layer of hidden units in turn, until the input and output match. The process is usually performed in small increments, and the mathematics are complicated.

backward propagation of errors *backward propagation.*

backward span A *short-term memory* task in which a list of items is presented to the subject, who must repeat them back in reverse order of presentation – a more sadistic form of the *ordered recall* task.

ballistic movement A movement in which, although the final destination is planned, the intervening stages are not closely monitored or controlled. See *servomechanism.*

bandwidth Term denoting the parameters under which a process can operate.

Bartlett tradition General term for research into qualitative rather than quantitative aspects of memory (e.g. *War of the Ghosts*).

BASEBALL *Artificial intelligence* programme which was a database of (not surprisingly) baseball information. The programme provided answers about baseball facts, provided they were presented in an acceptable phraseology.

baseline performance The performance at a 'basic' form of a task before any permutations on the task and/or training are given.

basic level category The level of generality at which people naturally tend to categorize an item. E.g. a horse tends to be named a 'horse' rather than a 'mammal' or a 'thoroughbred' (being respectively examples of more general and more specific labels). Rosch's *prototype theory* provides a greater level of justification for this. Items within a general category have relatively few features in common (e.g. the general category of 'plant life'). Conversely, items within a specific category have a great deal in common, but also share a lot of features in common with members of other categories on the same 'level' (e.g. 'roses' and 'carnations'). The basic level category is an intermediary, and generally represents the level at which there is the best balance between attributes of the specific and general levels.

basic problem space See *problem space*.

Baye's formula *Baye's theorem*.

Baye's theorem Formula expressing the probability that an event will occur because of a particular *mutually exclusive event*, rather than an alternative. E.g. suppose we know that disease X causes a certain type of rash in 90% of patients, but the same rash occurs in 20% of patients with disease Y and 7% of patients with disease Z. Baye's theorem can calculate the probability that a patient with this rash has each of the three diseases.

BDI *Beck Depression Inventory*.

Beck Depression Inventory (BDI) Widely-used self-report questionnaire, measuring depression. Because it is quick and easy to administer, the test has often been used in studies of the effects of emotional state on cognitive performance.

behaviourism In its rigid form, the belief that psychologists should only study what can be objectively measured. All voluntary acts can be seen as a response to some form of stimulation. Of the various stages in this process, the stimulus can be measured, as can the strength and/or appropriateness of the response, but the thought processes used to do

this cannot. Hence, behaviourism concentrated on the stimulus and response, and rigorously excluded discussion of mental processes. The theory had a very strong hold on psychology from the 1920s to the late 1950s, but was eventually recognized as being too limited in its scope, and researchers began to create models of mental processing.

belief bias Producing inaccurate results by relying on intuition and prior experience rather than logic.

beta (β) See *signal detection analysis*.

biconditional Term used in logic, corresponding to the English phrase 'if and only if'. In a statement 'if and only if A, then B', the statement is only correct if the terms are either both true or both false.

bigram A group of two letters.

bilabial (phonetics) Pertaining to a *phone* whose production involves the movements of both lips.

bilaterality (hemispheres) *functional symmetry*.

bilingual Possessing the ability to speak two languages. **Compound bilingualism** refers to subjects who learnt both languages simultaneously, whilst **coordinate bilingualism** refers to subjects who learnt one language after the other.

binocular depth cue See *monocular depth cue*.

biological plausibility The degree to which a model (typically, a *neurocomputational* model) accurately replicates or mimics known anatomical, physiological and/or other biological functions. See *ecological validity*.

bit See *information (H)*.

blackboard (1) Term sometimes used to denote a memory *buffer store*. (2) The term also denotes a process in some *artificial intelligence* programmes (e.g. *HEARSAY*), which collates information from several specialized processors to form an answer to the problem set.

blindsight Phenomenon observed in some neurological patients, who, although apparently blind, can respond to visual stimuli, although they are not consciously aware of their existence. This is usually attributed to some surviving visual connections with more 'primitive' areas of the brain.

BLIRNET A *network model* of word recognition. The acronym stands for 'Builds Location-Independent Representations Network'.

block (1) Group of subjects assigned together because of something they have in common. (2) Group of tests or other items, whose link is either that they are all given to the same subject, or that they are given in the same time period (the latter definition applies particularly to repetitious measures such as *reaction times*). For either definition, the source of the similarity is called the ***blocking factor***. (3) An item which appears unbidden when a subject is attempting to recall other items, and which prevents their recall (the *ugly sister effect* is an example of this).

block design test Sub-test of the *Wechsler* intelligence tests and other intelligence tests. The subject is required to replicate patterns using a set of blocks. As the test progresses, the designs become harder to replicate.

blocking factor See *block*.

body (syllable) *rime*.

BOSS The initial syllable of a word, as it is pronounced. The term is derived from the *BOSS model*. The initial syllable of a word as it appears *orthographically* (which may be at variance with the spoken BOSS) is called the ***oBOSS***.

BOSS model Model of *syllable* recognition (particularly the first syllable of the word), devised by Taft. The term is an acronym of 'Basic Orthographic Syllabic Structure'.

bottleneck Generally, the term is used to denote a mental process (particularly a model derived from *information processing*) in which there is more information to be processed than can be accommodated. This is akin to pouring liquid out of a narrow necked bottle (e.g. a wine bottle) in which the flow is slowed by the constriction of space through which it must pass. In pouring liquid, all will eventually come out. However, in the bottleneck analogy, it is argued that some of the information will often be lost before it can be processed. See *bottleneck theories*.

bottleneck theories A group of theories which argue that *selective attention* occurs by processing all incoming information to a certain extent, before the information channel which is to be attended to is selected for further processing. How much processing takes place before selection occurs is open to debate. The ***late bottleneck theories*** argue that a lot of processing occurs, the ***early bottleneck theories*** (not surprisingly) argue the reverse. The debate hinges on how much of the unattended information is recalled by subjects. E.g. if quite complex details of the supposedly unattended information can be recalled, then it is argued that a lot of processing has taken place before it was excluded (supporting the late bottleneck theory). By the same token, finding that little can be remembered supports the early bottleneck theory. See *filter*.

bottom layer (parallel distributed processing) See *layer (parallel distributed processing)*.

bottom-up processing Recognizing an item by identifying its component items and building them up into a coherent whole (e.g. reading a word letter-by-letter). See *top-down processing*.

bound morpheme *Morpheme* which is not in itself a word (e.g. 'il' in 'illegible'). See *root morpheme*.

boundary (of a set/concept) The criteria which determine to which set a 'borderline case' should belong (e.g. whether a certain ambiguous colour should be classified as green or blue).

brain trace Change in neurological structure/pattern of activation created in representing a memory.

brainstorming Session in which a group of people are encouraged to generate ideas, regardless of how inappropriate they are, in the hope of creating fresh approaches to a problem.

breakthrough See *dichotic listening task*.

Bridges of Konigsberg problem A problem involving the following topography. Between the two banks of a river there are two islands. One island has two bridges, one going to either bank. The other island has four bridges, two going to either bank. There is a further bridge, which joins the two islands. The task (which is impossible), is to start at any point and return to it, having crossed each bridge only once.

bridging inference *Inference* that new information refers to a topic previously encountered.

brightness masking See *masking*.

Broca's aphasia *Aphasia* whose principal symptom is an inability to speak. Contrast with *Wernicke's aphasia*.

Brodmann's Areas Division of *cerebral cortex* into forty-seven areas, based on differences in tissue structure.

Brown–Peterson task Named after its inventors (Brown and the Petersons conceived the idea roughly simultaneously at different institutions), the task presents subjects with a list of to-be-remembered items, then gives them a distracting task (usually counting backwards in units of two or three), before asking subjects to recall the to-be-remembered items. The task thus assesses the fragility of *short-term memory* and also measures *concurrent processing*.

brute force (problem solving) Method of problem solving in which every single permutation of combinations of moves is analysed to discover the best solution. This is is only feasible in humans for problems with a limited range of moves. The term usually applies to computer programmes which have the necessary processing power.

Buddhist monk problem A measure of problem-solving ability. Subjects are told the tale of a Buddhist monk who travels up a mountain on one day, and travels down it on another. The journey takes exactly the same time going up as it does coming down, and both journeys begin and end at exactly the same times of day. The subject has to prove that at one point the monk inevitably will be at the same place at the same time of day when ascending and descending.

buffer store A term adopted from computing. A temporary store of information, which is quickly erased unless revived or otherwise strengthened. The term is often used as a synonym for *short-term memory*.

C

CA *chronological age.*

calendar calculators (Rare) individuals who possess the ability to calculate mentally the day of the week upon which any given date in the past occurred.

canalization (-isation) A reduction in the range of possible behaviours or strategies.

candle problem See *functional fixedness.*

capacity, memory *memory capacity.*

capacity, mental *mental capacity.*

capacity model Any *mental model* (often of *attention*) which is concerned with how *mental capacity* is divided up between different sub-processes.

capacity sharing model See *postponement model.*

capture error Type of *slip of action* in which the person erroneously takes one (frequently used) course of action when another (less frequently used) one was intended.

carryover effect See *test wise subjects.*

Cartesian Pertaining to Descartes (see *Descartes' theory of mind*).

Cartesian dualism See *Descartes' theory of mind.*

cascade model A *mental model* in which processing units are arranged in a hierarchy – as soon as a low level unit is activated, it activates higher level units further along the processing chain.

case (letters) Describes whether letters are in capitals (*upper case*) or not (*lower case*). *Alternating case* refers to words made up of alternate upper and lower case letters. Thus, 'CASE' is in upper case, 'case' is in lower case, and 'CaSe' is in alternating case.

case frame See *case grammar.*

case grammar A representation of language in which units of language are categorized into 'cases' according to their semantic relationship with each other. The most often cited of these are: the *agentive case* (an animate entity who does the action); the *instrumental case* (an inanimate object involved in the action); the *recipient case* (an animate entity who receives the effects of the action); the *objective case* (an inanimate object affected by the action); and the *locative case* (the location of the action). Combinations of cases (i.e. representing sentences and phrases) are known as *case frames.*

CAT *Cognitive Abilities Test.*

CAT scan *computerized axial tomography.*

catch trials In measuring *absolute threshold*, a set of trials on which no stimulus is presented. If the subject claims to perceive a stimulus on some of these trials, then this bias towards positive responses can be used to weight scores of his/her performance when a very faint stimulus is present.

categorical perception (phonetics) The tendency to perceive an ambiguous *phoneme*-like sound as having one identity, (i.e. being a specific phoneme, rather than sharing features of two or more phonemes).

categorical syllogism *Syllogism* in which the items are expressed as members of categories (e.g. 'all As are B, all Bs are C; are all As members of C?').

categorization (-isation) test Any test in which subjects must place items into groups or categories. The measure can gauge an intellectual skill, or may be used simply to examine a specific problem with categorization (e.g. after brain damage). Compare with *category verification task*.

category mistake The assignation of a member of one class of items to another class.

category search Any model of mental functioning which assumes that organization of knowledge is based around categories, and that items are primarily processed according to which category they fall in, and how typical they are of the category in question.

category size effect The phenomenon whereby, under certain circumstances, subjects process information on items from a small category faster than items from a large category.

category specificity The degree to which an effect is confined to the processing of a particular category (e.g. in studies of brain damage, the degree to which damage is confined to the processing of one type of information).

category verification task Task in which subjects must decide if items are members of particular categories. Compare with *categorization test*.

Cattell Culture-Fair Test (CCFT) Commercial intelligence test, which by avoiding measures of linguistic skills and general knowledge, supposedly measures intellectual skills equally accessible to people of all cultural/linguistic backgrounds.

causal inference *Inference* of the consequences of a particular state of affairs or set of actions, and conversely, what set of affairs or actions might account for a particular outcome.

causal texture The general pattern of association between items and/or events.

CCC *consonant trigram.*

CCC trigram *consonant trigram.*

CCFT *Cattell Culture-Fair Test .*

CD *conceptual dependency.*

ceiling effect Effect achieved by giving a group a test which is too easy – an undesirably large proportion of group members scores full or nearly full marks, making discrimination between them impossible. See *floor effect.*

central aphasia *conduction aphasia.*

central controller *central processor.*

central executive See *working memory.*

central process In certain *mental models,* the term refers to any process which is involved in all or most operations performed by the model. This is contrasted with **peripheral processes,** which only operate under certain more specialized conditions.

central processor A *processing unit* which supervises and controls the activities of other processing units. One of its functions is **resource allocation**. Since the mind has a limited *mental capacity,* there is only a finite amount of 'mental energy' available to run mental operations. The central processor is held to be responsible for allocating the capacity available to each operation. In many models, how the central processor makes its decisions is not adequately explored, leading to hypotheses of a *homunculus* in the system.

central task *primary task.*

cerebral cortex Usually known by its abbreviated name of *cortex*. The cerebral cortex is the characteristic wrinkled surface of the brain. It is divided into two linked *hemispheres* and can be divided into four regions or lobes (see *frontal, parietal, occipital* and *temporal lobes*) which have different functions. The cerebral cortex is responsible for the majority of higher intellectual functions.

CFF (1) *critical flicker fusion.* (2) *critical fusion flicker.*

CFQ *Cognitive Failures Questionnaire.*

characteristic attribute *characteristic feature.*

characteristic feature See *defining feature.*

cheap necklace problem Test of problem-solving ability. Subjects are given the following problem (which has been Anglicized): there are four pieces of chain each comprising three links. It costs two pence to open a link and three pence to close it. How can the four pieces of chain be joined together in a circle for no more than fifteen pence?

childhood amnesia The loss of memories from early childhood which is disproportionately greater than would be predicted from simple forgetfulness. Originally thought (e.g. by Freud) to be due to suppression of emotionally fraught memories, more recent explanations have taken a cognitive approach (e.g. young children are intellectually incapable of storing memories efficiently, so they are forgotten).

Chinese readers and spellers
People who read and spell by the visual shape of the word, without paying much attention to what it sounds like. Compare with *Phoenecian readers and spellers.*

Chinese Room Illustration of a criticism of *strong AI* by Searle (philosopher). A monolingual English speaker is placed in a room with the task of answering questions (in writing) about a story written in Chinese. The person is provided with a set of rules for processing (but not translating) the Chinese symbols (Chinese is a *logographic writing* system) and, by following a set procedure, a response (in the form of Chinese logographs) can be made. The person can thus make as accurate a response as a Chinese speaker, and anyone who did not know who was in the room would be unable to judge whether or not the person was a speaker of Chinese. However, the person in the room has at no point an understanding of the meaning of the symbols s/he is processing. Searle argues that an *artificial intelligence* programme is like this – it can accurately imitate the workings of a mind, but there is no conscious awareness of what it is doing.

choice reaction time (CRT) See *reaction time.*

Chomsky's theory of language
Linguist Noam Chomsky first proposed in the the 1950s that all languages possess the same **deep structure**. I.e., although languages obviously differ in their immediate appearance or **surface structure** (their phonetics, syntax, etc.), they all can be transformed (hence the term **transformational grammar**) to the same essential relationship of *noun phrases* and *verb phrases*, and from these, meaning can be extracted. Chomsky felt that knowledge of the deep structures was innate, and without such a **language acquisition device (LAD)**, a child could not learn a language. This was in opposition to the *behaviourist* model of lan-

guage acquisition, which argued that learning took place by simple association. Chomsky's work is widely quoted, although some of his more extreme views have been criticized. In historical terms, his work is important because it was a significant counter-attack to the *behaviourism* movement.

chronological age (CA) The length of time a person has been alive.

chronometric analysis Any measure of mental processes which is primarily interested in the time taken to complete processes. Inter alia, the time taken is held to be indicative of the complexity of the process. See *subtraction method.*

chunk Term devised by Miller (see *Magical Number Seven*) to denote a basic processing/memory unit. The composition of a chunk varies according to the prior knowledge of the subject. E.g. consider the list '2014266977'. If the subject recognized the list as comprising the telephone numbers of two friends (e.g. '20142' was one such number, and '66977' the other) then the list could be reduced to two chunks. However, if the subject did not have this prior information, then the list would simply be a list of ten individual numbers, or ten separate chunks. Similarly, the word 'schadenfreude' is one chunk if one understands German, but is a collection of thirteen separate letters/chunks if one cannot. The mechanisms by which chunking works, and what constitutes a 'chunk' have been debated, although the process, at least at a descriptive level, has been widely accepted.

chunking The process of creating *chunks.* The technique is sometimes taught in an effort to enhance memorization skills.

circadian rhythm A cycle of mental and physical changes repeating itself approximately once every twenty-four hours.

Clive Wearing A patient with very severe *amnesia* following an attack of encephalitis. He is celebrated not because of the uniqueness of his symptoms, but because of a justly celebrated television documentary about him called 'A Prisoner of Consciousness'.

close-ended question Question for which there is only a limited range of answers to choose from (typically, 'yes' and 'no'). This is contrasted with an *open-ended question*, in which the subject can respond with a wide (and often, in theory, infinite) range.

closed class word *function word.*

closed loop processes *Attentional processes.* See also *open loop processes.*

closed node *Node* which has been processed.

closed scenario *close-ended question.*

closed set (knowledge) A group of facts which cannot be added to (e.g. the list of nineteenth century British monarchs). Compare with *open set (knowledge).*

closed system A system unaffected by external forces.

cloze procedure Reading test method – subjects have to insert appropriate words into blanks in a passage of text (e.g. fill in the blank in 'the cat sat on…mat'). The term is meant to indicate a link with the *Gestalt* concept of closure (the hypothesized drive to mentally fill in missing gaps in an image).

clustering The phenomenon whereby related items in a group of to-be-remembered items tend to be remembered together, and in *free recall*, tend to be recalled together.

clustering in recall *clustering.*

CM *consistent mapping.*

coarse coding The phenomenon whereby the same item can be produced/*encoded* when processing several different concepts.

cocktail party phenomenon A term with two quite different meanings. (1) The phenomenon whereby, at a party or other large social gathering, it is possible to hold a conversation which apparently has your full attention, and yet you can detect when someone else mentions your name, or other details about you. This is an elegant demonstration that *unattended information* is processed more deeply than some researchers would choose to argue. (2) The phenomenon whereby, at a party or other large social gathering, it is possible to hold a conversation which you can concentrate on, in spite of the large number of other conversations going on around you, competing for your attention. This is an elegant demonstration that *unattended information* is processed less deeply than some researchers would choose to argue.

code switching Shifting from one language or dialect to another.

coding *encoding.*

cogito ergo sum See *Descartes' theory of mind.*

cognition (1) The understanding, acquisition and processing of knowledge, or, more loosely, thought processes. (2) The study of the same.

cognitive Pertaining to *cognition.*

Cognitive Abilities Test (CAT) Intelligence test battery, with a chief subdivision into nonverbal and verbal measures.

cognitive approach General term for any method which uses ideas and/or techniques derived from *cognition.*

cognitive architecture A *mental model* which attempts to explain the very basic processes underlying cognitive acts.

cognitive capacity *mental capacity.*

cognitive economy The theory that information is stored as compactly and conveniently as possible. E.g. rather than separately encoding the same information about every single person one knows (that s/he is human, a mammal, a living being, etc.), this information is stored once, and knowledge about people is stored in a 'people category', which shares access to this general set of properties.

cognitive effort At its simplest, the amount of effort put into performing a mental process. The term often more specifically applies to the amount of *mental capacity* required to perform a process.

Cognitive Failures Questionnaire (CFQ) A test devised by Broadbent, which asks subjects to report instances of memory failure in recent everyday life (e.g. forgetting to buy items when shopping, etc.). Used to assess how forgetful people are in 'real life' (compared with more artificial laboratory tasks).

cognitive interview Technique for maximizing recall in *eyewitness memory.*

cognitive map A mental representation of a spatial array (e.g. a route, a way through a maze, etc.).

cognitive miser The concept that subjects will attempt to exercise *cognitive* *economy* as much as possible. The term is used more often in social psychology than in cognition.

cognitive neuropsychology The study of cognitive functioning and it relationship to brain anatomy and processes. Typically, this involves studying patients suffering from brain damage which has marred intellectual performance. The pattern of deficits can indicate how cognition normally occurs.

cognitive neuroscience The study of cognitive functioning in terms of brain structure and function.

cognitive overload Processing a quantity of information which exceeds *mental capacity*.

cognitive penetrability The ease with which a cognitive process is affected by expectations of how it should work. The term was devised by Pylyshyn, who felt that certain processes were difficult or impossible to affect by expectations of how they should work (this is debatable). These 'impenetrable' functions are sometimes called the *functional architecture*.

cognitive psychology *cognition*.

cognitive psychophysiology The study of the interaction between cognitive skills and physiological processes.

cognitive restructuring Replacing 'faulty' ideas and concepts with new and 'better' ones. The term is largely limited to therapeutic situations.

cognitive revolution Semi-serious term for the rise in academic popularity of *cognition* (and more specifically, the study of *mental models*) during the 1960s, and the concomitant decline in the popularity of *behaviourism*.

cognitive science (1) The examination of cognitive processes by means of mathematical or (more usually) computer modelling. (2) More loosely, *cognition*. (3) Yet more loosely, the study of knowledge and its uses.

cognitive space model See *levels of processing*.

cognitive stage (skill acquisition) In some models of skill acquisition, the first stage, in which the subject learns the facts necessary to perform the skill. This is followed by the *associative stage*, in which the subject refines his/her actions, eliminating errors in their execution, and attains a deeper memory of them. The final, *autonomous stage* occurs when the actions become an *automatic process*.

cognitive style A problem-solving method or method of intellectual functioning consistently used by a subject.

cognitive therapy It can be argued that many mentally ill patients misinterpret events so that they 'feed' the illness (e.g. a person afraid of rejection will take the slightest negative comment as further 'proof' that they are unlovable). Cognitive therapy attempts to make patients realize, through self-analysis and various exercises, that the majority of events can be explained in a rational and non-negative manner (i.e. the therapy tries to restore common sense to the patient).

cohort A group of people raised in the same environment and/or period of time. Almost invariably refers to a group of people of similar age.

cohort effect A difference between age groups which is better attributed to differences in the ways they were raised, educated, etc., than to their ages per se.

combinatorial explosion Phenomenon whereby in any problem in which each stage/move yields a multiple range of choices (e.g. chess), the range of choices increases at a very rapid rate, the more steps ahead one considers. E.g. the range of possible moves in chess or draughts is fairly limited when looking for one's next move. However, if one considers five or six moves ahead, then the total possible choice of moves is numbered in millions.

commissive *Speech act* in which the speaker promises to do something.

common fate Phenomenon observed by the *Gestalt* school, whereby items which have the same motion tend to be seen as features of the same object.

common ground (linguistics) The assumption that the speaker and listener share sufficient background knowledge for speech to be intelligible.

compensatory model *Mental model* (almost always an *interactive model*) which argues that weaker processes can be compensated for by other processes working harder/faster.

compensatory tracking See *tracking*.

competence The hypothesized 'real' state of a subject's abilities. Due to errors of measurement, etc., a subject's test performance may be an imperfect measure of his or her competence.

competence (linguistics) *linguistic competence*.

competitive learning nets (parallel distributed processing) A form of *neural network* which 'teaches' itself to find sources of similarity and difference between items with which it is supplied.

completion rate (1) The rate at which a task is completed. (2) The proportion of the total original sample which completes all the tests.

completion test Any measure in which the subject must complete an item (e.g.

an incomplete sentence, a shape with a section missing, etc.).

complex reaction time *choice reaction time*.

composition In the *ACT* model, the creation of complex *productions* from simpler ones.

compound bilingualism See *bilingualism*.

compound reaction time *choice reaction time*.

compound word Word formed from two or more *morphemes*. A *pseudocompound word* is one in which a segment looks like a morpheme, but is not (e.g. 'his' in 'history'). The segments of a pseudocompound word are called *pseudomorphemes*.

comprehension test (1) A measure of ability to understand an item (typically, a passage of text). (2) A *crystallized intelligence* measure of knowing the correct things to do in particular circumstances (e.g. 'what should you do if you cut your finger?').

computational metaphor of the mind See *metaphor of mental functioning*.

computer analogy The use of computing terminology, particularly of programmes and programming language, as a metaphor of mental functioning.

computer simulation (CS) See *artificial intelligence*.

computerized axial tomography (CAT scan) A body scan by means of a sequence of highly sensitive X-rays, which display successive cross-sections of the body.

computerized transaxial tomography (CT) *computerized axial tomography*.

concept-driven processing *top-down processing*.

concept formation The creation of a rule defining membership of a concept, from examples of the said concept.

concept identification *concept formation.*

concept learning *concept formation.*

conceptual coherence The degree to which members of a concept are subjectively felt to be akin to each other.

conceptual dependencies (CD) Term devised by Schank to denote the relationship between the *semantic primitives* produced as a result of a semantic analysis of a statement.

conceptual organization (-isation) The ability to treat items at an abstract level in order to uncover basic rules and principles.

conceptual peg A method of thinking (typically, a strong mental image) which helps in the processing and/or remembering of information.

conceptually-driven processing *top-down processing.*

concordance doctrine *doctrine of concordance.*

concrete image Mental image which is recalled with a strong sensation of its physical properties.

concrete intelligence See *abstract intelligence.*

concrete object Item which has a physical identity (as opposed to e.g. an abstract concept).

concurrent articulation A type of *concurrent processing* task – subjects must talk (usually repeating a short nonsensical phrase) while performing another task. It particularly disrupts tasks requiring verbal processing.

concurrent processing *secondary task procedure.*

concurrent tasks Experimental method in which the subject is required to do two or more tasks simultaneously.

conditional probability Given a particular set of information, the probability that a particular state exists (e.g. if an animal has spots and big teeth, the probability that it is a leopard rather than e.g. a vampire with measles). See *cue validity.*

conditional reasoning Reasoning using the basic proposition of 'if A then B', where 'A' is called the **antecedent**, and 'B' the **consequent**.

conduction aphasia *Aphasia* characterized by an inability to repeat words, although other aspects of language are relatively normal.

confabulation Condition in which the subject makes up stories or other implausible explanations to cover up gaps in his/her memory or other skills. Generally, the term is reserved for brain-damaged patients where there is no conscious attempt to deceive.

configural superiority effect The phenomenon whereby many stimuli are more easily recognized/processed in some configurations than in others.

confirmation bias The tendency to search for evidence supporting a theory, rather than looking for negative evidence to disprove it (see *falsifiability*).

confounding The simultaneous change of two or more variables, so that any subsequent changes in another variable cannot be unambiguously attributed to just one of the first-named variables. E.g. if wages are increased by 100% at the same time as the workplace temperature is raised by three degrees, it would be difficult to ascribe a subsequent increase in productivity purely to the change in temperature.

confusion matrix A record of a subject's responses used in some recognition tasks. The matrix, or chart, records how often the subject correctly identifies a stimulus, and, when s/he is wrong, which stimulus is erroneously selected instead. The errors can provide experimenters with an indication of what features of the stimulus the subject is attending to. E.g. in a letter recognition task, subjects might, when they misidentify 'B', often choose 'P' or 'R', rather than, e.g., 'M' or 'K'. This might indicate that subjects are attending to the curved segments of the letter, rather than the straight vertical line.

confusions/blends Types of *slips of action* where items needed in one process are used (inappropriately) in another (e.g. writing with a chocolate bar and putting a pen in one's mouth).

congruent priming See *priming*.

conjunctive concept A category which is identified by the presence of a particular set of characteristics. This contrasts with a *disjunctive concept*, in which several different permutations of characteristics represent the same category (e.g. the concept of 'games' can be represented in many ways).

connectionism (1) Theory proposed by Thorndike at the turn of the twentieth century that learning was by trial and error, and that as learning progressed, the errors diminished, thereby honing the skill to accuracy. (2) Alternative term for *parallel distributed processing*, by extension from definition (1).

connectionist network Model of intellectual functioning which employs *connectionism*.

consciousness Possessing awareness of oneself and one's internal and external environments (in particular, awareness of one's psychological processes). The issue in recent times has aroused interest through the debate over *strong AI* (see also *Chinese Room* and *Descartes' theory of mind*).

consequent See *conditional reasoning*.

conservative focusing In problem-solving or *concept formation*, examining one feature of the problem at a time. This is in contrast with *focus gambling*, in which several features are examined simultaneously.

consistency (spelling) The extent to which other words sharing the same groupings of letters have the same pronunciation of those letters (e.g. 'bat' and 'cat' are *consistent words*, whilst 'hint' and 'pint' are *inconsistent words*). See *regular spelling*.

consistency effect The phenomenon whereby *consistent words* are pronounced with a faster *latency* than *inconsistent words*. See *regularity effect*.

consistent analogy (spelling) See *pronunciation by analogy*.

consistent mapping (CM) In a *memory search, visual search*, or similar paradigm, a condition in which the *distractors* clearly belong to a different category than that of the targets (e.g. in searching for letters, all the distractors are in numbers). This is an easier task than *varied mapping (VM)*, in which the targets and distractors share features in common (e.g. the targets are vowels and the distractors are consonants). An even harder permutation of this is *reverse mapping (RM)*, in which items which previously were distractors are now to be treated as targets, and vice versa.

consistent words See *consistency (spelling)*.

consonant trigram (CCC) See *trigram*.

consonant–vowel–consonant trigram *CVC trigram*.

constituent (psycholinguistics) A unit of a sentence expressing a key idea and/or process. The rule typically cited is that a constituent can be replaced by a single word without loss of meaning. This 'core meaning' is also known as the *ultimate constituent*.

constraint seeking strategy In solving a problem (e.g. in a 'twenty questions' game), seeking answers which progressively reduce the set size of all possible answers.

constructive model (memory) (1) Model which argues that memories of complex ideas can be formed from the conjunction of simpler ideas, and that specific simpler memories may be lost in the process. (2) *constructivist theory*.

constructivist theory Theory of memory/perception founded by Bartlett which argues that we use prior knowledge to shape our memories to fit in with how we expect the world to be. See *schema theory*.

content-addressable memory Any memory store which can be accessed by its contents. This means that a specific item can be retrieved without having to search through the whole of the memory store. It also implies that once one piece of information has been found, other related items from the same store can also be accessed.

content words Words whose primary purpose is to provide meaning, rather than *syntax* (e.g. nouns, adjectives, verbs, etc.). See *function words*.

contention scheduling A hypothesized process controlling *partially automatic*

processing. The choice of which of a range of alternative actions should be taken is based upon perceptions and priorities, without the intervention of conscious decision-making.

context-dependency (memory) The degree to which retrieval of a memory is dependent upon the context in which it was first acquired. E.g. if you have learnt something whilst in room A, how easy will it be to remember it when in room B or room C? If the information can only be satisfactorily recalled in room A, then the information would be said to be highly context-dependent (and if it can be recalled anywhere, then it would be said to be *context-independent*). *State-dependency* refers to the degree to which retrieval is dependent upon the subject's internal state. E.g. some studies have shown that subjects remembered information which they had learnt when drunk better when they were drunk again than when they were sober (and similarly, soberly-learnt material was better recalled when sober than when drunk).

context-dependent grammar Grammatical structure which is determined by the context of the statement in question. In contrast, *context-free grammar* is not shaped by context.

context-dependent information The phenomenon whereby some information about an item is only recalled or processed under certain circumstances. See *context-dependency (memory)*.

context-dependent rules (linguistics) *context-dependent grammar*.

context effect The degree to which the context in which an item is encountered affects its processing (e.g. one is more likely to remember a rhino encountered in a kitchen than in a wildlife film).

context-free grammar See *context-dependent grammar.*

context-free rules (linguistics) *context-free grammar.*

context independent (memory) See *context dependency (memory).*

context memory Memory for the context in which the to-be-remembered item was learnt. Baddeley suggests that the context can be of two types. In *interactive context memory*, the context affects how the to-be-remembered item is memorized (e.g. the word 'skin' has different meanings when seen in the contexts of sunbathing and hunting). In *independent context memory*, the context has no effect on how the to-be-remembered item is remembered.

context-sensitive grammar *context- dependent grammar.*

contextual effects The manner in which the context in which an item is presented can affect its identification. E.g. it would be easier to identify a badly written three letter word as 'cat' presented in the sentence 'the XXX sat on the mat' than presented in isolation.

contextual interference Impairment in performance caused by the context in which the performance takes place (typically, the term refers to interference caused by having to perform two or more separate tasks in the same test session).

contingency judgement Judging whether there is a relationship between items and/or events.

contingency matrix Table indicating the probable response/behaviour of a subject under a variety of conditions (e.g. if conditions are Y, the probability that the subject will do A rather than B compared with when conditions are X).

continuation problem Measure of problem-solving skill, in which the subject must provide the next item(s) in a sequence. E.g. '1 3 9 27 ?').

continuous motor skill Motor skill in which the subject must make continuous adjustments to activity (e.g. running, driving, etc.) to compensate for deviations. This contrasts with *discrete motor skills*, in which an individual action is performed as one complete unit (e.g. throwing a ball, writing a single letter, etc.).

continuous recognition task *Shepard and Teightsoonian recognition paradigm.*

continuous representation *analogue representation.*

control processes In *mental models* (particularly those based on *information processing*), the processes responsible for moving items from one memory store/processing mechanism to another and for regulating the sub-processes.

control theory Theory of functioning which emphasizes the role of *feedback* in monitoring and executing performance. See *feedback signal.*

controlled process *attentional process*, definition (2).

convenient viewing location (reading) See *preferred viewing location (reading).*

convenient viewing position (reading) *convenient viewing location (reading).*

convergent thinking See *divergent thinking.*

conversion hypothesis Theory that subjects make certain types of errors in *syllogisms* because they fail to convert the arguments in a logically acceptable manner.

convolution (parallel distributed processing) A method by which a *neural net* can represent and retrieve stored representations.

cooperative principle The argument that both speaker and listener follow and expect the *Gricean maxims* in conversation.

coordinate bilingualism See *bilingualism*.

copy cue Term devised by Tulving to denote how a subject *recognizes* an item, because the item is a copy of his/her memory and vice versa.

corpus callosum The principal anatomical link between the left and right *hemispheres* of the brain.

Corsi blocks task A test of visuo-spatial memory. Subjects are shown an array of blocks positioned on a table. The experimenter taps on some of these blocks in a sequence which the subject is asked to copy. The experimenter gradually increases the length of sequence until the subject's *memory span* is discovered.

cortex *cerebral cortex*.

cortical Pertaining to the *cerebral cortex*.

covert speech *inner speech*.

creativity Largely synonymous with *divergent thinking*. The term generally refers to any ability to produce novel ideas. Note that the term has a less 'dramatic' meaning than the layperson's use – i.e. it is not confined to great artists, writers, etc.

creativity test Any measure of ability to produce original ideas. Usually there are caveats that the ideas should be plentiful and feasible. See *divergent thinking*.

criterion *response criterion*.

critical flicker fusion (CFF) The slowest rate at which a flickering light is perceived as a 'continuous' light. See *two flash fusion*.

critical fusion flicker (CFF) *critical flicker fusion*.

cross-modal Across the senses. E.g. in *cross-modal transfer*, an object which has previously only been encountered by one sensory system can be recognized in another (e.g. an object previously only touched can be recognized by sight).

cross-modal transfer See *cross-modal*.

cross talk The erroneous perception of features in an item which in fact belong to other items presented simultaneously or within a short period of time of the item in question.

CRT (1) *choice reaction time*. (2) cathode ray tube.

crystallized intelligence The amount of factual (as opposed to autobiographical) knowledge a person has acquired during a lifetime – roughly corresponds to the lay term 'general knowledge'.

CS *computer simulation*.

CT *computerized transaxial tomography*.

cube problem (visual imagery) Subjects are asked to imagine a cube which is painted blue on two opposite sides, and red on the other four. If the cube is divided into twenty-seven equally-sized smaller cubes, how many of the smaller cubes will have red and blue sides?

cue (1) Any item or action which aids the retrieval of a memory (e.g. as in *cued recall*). (2) More generally, any item or action which serves to prompt the subject to perform a particular action.

cue competition When the subject has two or more cues for an item or different items, the process whereby the subject selects the cues upon which his/her decision will be based.

cue-dependent forgetting The theory that memories which can no longer be retrieved are still stored, but the *cues* which will retrieve them have been lost.

cue failure Failure effectively to use the information provided by a *cue*.

cue validity In Rosch's *prototype theory*, a measure of how representative a particular attribute is of a particular category (e.g. if an item is said to have the attribute of tasting savoury, then this has a high cue validity for vegetables, but a low cue validity for fruit).

cued recall The process of retrieving a memory in which the subject is aided by being provided with partial features of the to-be-retrieved item(s), such as the first letter, words which sound like it, etc. See *recall*.

cued recall task See *recall task*.

cueing Any experimental process in which the subject's performance is manipulated using *cues* (e.g. *cued recall*).

culture-fair test Test which is equally fair to all subjects, no matter what their cultural background (e.g. *Cattell Culture-Fair Test*). See *culture-specific test*.

culture-free test *culture-fair test*.

culture-specific test Test which is specifically targeted at individuals from one (usually minority) culture. See *culture-fair test*.

curve of forgetting *forgetting curve*.

CV Group of two letters formed from a consonant and a vowel (e.g. 'da').

CVC *CVC trigram*.

CVC trigram See *trigram*.

cyclic model of perception Neisser's model of *object recognition*, in which there is a constant interplay between

bottom-up processing and *top-down processing* (roughly speaking, the bottom-up processing provides the raw information, and the top-down processing guides the bottom-up processing in searching for subsequent features).

cytoarchitecture The anatomical organization of cells (particularly in the brain).

D

d' See *signal detection analysis*.

d prime *d'*.

DACs *divided attention costs*.

Dani tribe A 'primitive' tribe from Papua New Guinea, who, amongst other attributes, have only two words for colours ('dark' and 'light'). There is evidence that they can discriminate between colours almost as well as Western subjects, thus providing a strong rebuttal of the 'strong' version of the *linguistic relativity hypothesis*.

data-driven error Type of *slip of action* where a person begins to perform one task, but the stimuli distract him or her into performing another. See also *goal switches*.

data-driven processing *bottom-up processing*.

data-limited process Process whose outcome is erroneous/incomplete because of the poor quality of the data it has operated upon. See *process deficiency* and *resource-limited process*.

D.B. Pseudonym of the patient whose symptoms and behaviour were reported in an often-cited case study of *blindsight*.

DCRT *discrete choice reaction time*.

deadline technique *response-signal technique*.

decay Loss of memorized information due to the passage of time, rather than displacement by new material. Contrast with *interference*.

decision theory Any method of studying how decisions are made.

declarative *Speech act* in which the speaker aims to give the listener a new piece of information.

declarative knowledge *declarative memory*.

declarative memory The mental storage of basic facts (e.g. 'New York is in the USA', 'Margaret Thatcher was once Prime Minister', etc.). Compare with *experiential knowledge/memory* and *procedural knowledge/memory*.

declarative network *semantic network*.

deductive inference *deductive reasoning*.

deductive reasoning *Inference* of the relationship between items from their similarities and differences with 'mutual associates' (e.g. (a) x=y, y=z: therefore, x=z; (b) dogs have fur, reptiles do not have fur, therefore dogs are not reptiles). By contrast, *inductive reasoning* is the formation of a general rule from a collection of observations (e.g. bees fly, butterflies fly, wasps fly, therefore all animals with wings can fly).

deep In cognition, the term usually refers to the underlying structure of an item or situation, rather than its surface appearance (although that may also be analysed); the *deep processing* of an item or situation would involve the analysis of the underlying structure. E.g. the deep processing of a word might attend to its meaning. Contrast with *shallow*.

deep dysgraphia A profound writing difficulty akin to *deep dyslexia* – patients have great difficulty in spelling new or *nonsense words*, and tend to write down words which are synonyms of the words they are supposed to be writing.

deep dyslexia An *acquired dyslexia* in which patients cannot read new or *non-sense words* (see *phonological dyslexia*) and also misread words for words of similar meaning.

deep processing See *deep*.

deep structure (1) See *Chomsky's theory of language*. (2) *deep*.

default assignment Assigning a *default value* to an item, because the true information is not available, has been forgotten, etc.

default value In the absence of any other information, the most probable form one would predict an item to have. The value created by a *default assignment*.

defining attribute *defining feature*.

defining feature A feature of an item which must be present for it to be a member of a category. This contrasts with a **characteristic feature**, which is present in many members of the category, but is not necessary for membership (e.g. in the category of birds, a defining feature is possession of wings, but the ability to fly is only a characteristic feature).

definition (of problem) The degree to which the *initial state* and *goal state* of a problem are specified. E.g. a problem such as 'tie the three pieces of rope together to make a longer rope' is well defined, whilst 'use any three items in the room to make an aesthetically pleasing objet d'art' is ill-defined.

degradation technique Any experimental technique in which the quality of the presentation of a stimulus (e.g. the clarity with which it can be seen) is reduced.

degraded stimulus Stimulus produced by *degradation technique*.

delayed response Any experimental technique in which the subject is shown a stimulus, and then is held back from giving his/her response for a certain period of time.

Delta rule (parallel distributed processing) Essentially, a rule governing the rate at which the strength of connections between items in a *neural network* can change; a rule for 'teaching' a *neural network* a particular pattern of activation. In certain circumstances, the desired output from a network is known; the Delta rule specifies how the activation from a network should increase if it falls below the desired output, and decrease if it is above it. This procedure proceeds by trial and error until the correct solution is hit upon. Note that no assumptions of a *homunculus*-like control are assumed − the process follows a basic rule, but does so blindly. See *Hebbian rules*.

demand characteristics (1) Features of an experiment which may bias a subject to perform in a particular way. (2) *affordances*.

demented dyslexia A condition found in some demented patients, who can read aloud perfectly normally, and yet have no understanding of what they are reading.

demons See *Pandemonium model*.

denial of the antecedent In *conditional reasoning*, erroneously concluding that the *consequent* must be false because the *antecedent* is. See *affirmation of the consequent*.

dental (phonetics) Pertaining to a *phone* whose production involves pressing the tongue against the front teeth.

denying the antecedent *denial of the antecedent*.

deontic Pertaining to that which is morally/socially acceptable.

depth of processing *levels of processing.*

derivational error Misreading or misspelling a word for another with the same semantic root (e.g. 'large' instead of 'largely'). The former is also called a *derivational reading error*, and the latter a *derivational spelling error.*

derivational reading error See *derivational error.*

derivational spelling error See *derivational error.*

Descartes' theory of mind René Descartes (1591–1650), philosopher and mathematician. His most famous argument – *cogito ergo sum* (usually translated as 'I think, therefore I am') – asserts that because one has awareness of one's own thoughts, then one can be certain of one's own existence. For example, it is possible that one is deceived about everything (a modern illustration of this concept is that one could be nothing more than a brain in the laboratory of a 'mad professor' which is being stimulated by electrical currents into believing that it is e.g. playing tennis). However, argued Descartes, even if deceived of everything else, one cannot deny that one has a feeling that it is oneself who is thinking (e.g. one would be aware that it was oneself playing tennis). Descartes addressed the *mind–body problem*, arguing in favour of *dualism* (or **Cartesian dualism** as it is named in his honour) – the belief that the mind and the brain are separate entities. The argument can be seen in terms of the 'cogito' argument – because if awareness of oneself can exist independently, however much one is deceived about everything else, then the mind 'must' be independent of bodily processes (in-

cluding the physical brain). How the non-corporeal mind can make itself known to the physical body was not resolved by Descartes (in later life, he cited the pineal gland in the brain as the meeting place of mind and brain) nor, indeed, by anyone since.

descender See *ascender.*

design features The features of a process (typically language) held to be absolutely necessary for its functioning.

detection task Any task in which the subject must detect the presence of a stimulus. Note that the subject often does not have to name the stimulus, or provide many details about it (or indeed be consciously aware of its features) before making the response.

detection theory *signal detection theory.*

detection threshold *absolute threshold.*

detectives and criminals problem See *river crossing problem.*

detour problem Any type of problem-solving task in which the correct solution is to take a 'detour', because the apparently most direct method does not work. E.g. when told to go from A to B in the fastest time possible, there may be two paths – a direct one across a swamp and a longer route along a road. The correct solution may be to take the longer route because one would sink in the swamp.

developmental aphasia A congenital failure of language. In its 'pure' form, it refers to a condition in which the child suffers delayed speech and linguistic skills in general, which cannot be attributed to hearing impairment, damaged vocal cords, mental retardation, autism, or environmental factors (e.g. having suffered extreme parental neglect). However, the term is often used to denote congenital language failure, regardless of whether other symptoms are present.

developmental dysgraphia A profound difficulty in spelling and writing and in learning to spell and write.

developmental dyslexia A profound difficulty in reading and in learning to read, which the afflicted person appears to have been born with. *Developmental dysgraphia* almost always appears in conjunction with it.

dialogue system *Artificial intelligence* programme in which the programme replies to questions and statements provided by a (usually human, though possibly another computer) subject.

diary study (1) Method used to assess a particular aspect of a person's activity for the purposes of research and/or therapy (e.g. recording how much and what type of food is eaten, etc.). (2) Method of assessing *autobiographical memory*. Subjects complete a diary, and they are subsequently asked what they can recall of particular events, days, etc. (3) Study of contents of a person's diaries, for changes in writing style, topics of interest, etc., as the person ages.

dichotic listening task Experimental procedure in which the subject receives aural messages to both ears simultaneously, and is instructed to attend to the input in a particular way. In the *split span procedure*, subjects are required to recall the information they have heard. This is either determined temporally (i.e. the information is recalled in the order it was heard, regardless of which ear received it) or by which ear heard it (i.e. all the information heard in one ear is recalled before the information heard in the other). The task can also be used as a measure of *selective attention* – e.g.

the subject must attend to information arriving at one ear only. Typically, the subject is required to *shadow* the information arriving in one ear, or has to recall information from one ear only. **Breakthrough** is said to occur when information from an unattended channel is (erroneously) processed.

dictionary *mental lexicon.*

dictionary units Representations of words within a *mental lexicon.*

difference reduction General term for problem-solving methods which seek to reduce the difference between the *initial state* and the *goal state.*

difference threshold See *threshold.*

digit cancellation Task in which the subject is presented with a display of numbers, and must strike out all examples of a particular number or group of numbers.

digit span See *span.*

digit string A sequence of numbers (typically, numbers used in a memory task).

digit-symbol substitution task (DSST) A measure of *fluid intelligence.* The subject is shown letters or numbers paired with patterns or shapes. Given a sequence of letters/numbers or patterns, the subject must identify their matches as quickly and accurately as possible.

digraph A *phoneme* represented by two letters (e.g. 'ph').

direct dyslexia *demented dyslexia.*

direct perception *Gibson's theory of direct perception.*

direct reading *visual reading.*

direct recall/recognition Immediately recalling/recognizing an item without any apparent intermediate steps. This contrasts with *indirect recall/recognition*, in which the recall/recognition occurs after performing some interme-diary processing.

direct route reading *visual reading.*

directed forgetting Instructing subjects to try to forget a specified set of pre-viously-encountered items. The degree to which the *to-be-forgotten (TBF)* items have been forgotten can later be assessed with a memory test.

directed thinking Thinking directed to-wards a specific purpose.

directive *Speech act* in which the speaker attempts to make the listener re-spond/perform a request. See *indirect directive.*

disconfirming the consequent *modus tollens.*

discrete choice reaction time (DCRT) See *reaction time.*

discrete motor skill See *continuous motor skill.*

discrete processing Process in which one stage must be totally complete before the next can begin.

discrete reaction time (DRT) See *reaction time.*

discrete representation *propositional rep-resentation.*

discrete simple reaction time (DSRT) See *reaction time.*

discriminability *sensitivity.*

discrimination failure *confusions/blends.*

disjunctive concept See *conjunctive con-cept.*

displacement (linguistics) The capacity of a language to refer to items which are not present at the time.

display set The total collection of items which can be presented to the subject.

distance effect (visual imagery) The phenomenon whereby, in scanning a mental image, it takes longer to 'move'

between items which are further apart than it does to move between items which are closer together.

distinctive feature (1) A feature of an item which distinguishes it from another. (2) In phonetics, a feature which some pho-nemes possess whilst others do not (e.g. *voiced* versus *unvoiced,* etc.).

distinctiveness model Model of memory which argues that items are better re-membered if they are encoded as dis-tinct from each other.

distracter *distractor.*

distractibility The ease with which a sub-ject's *attention* wanders from a task.

distractor *distractor item.*

distractor item An item which is not one for which the subject is searching (i.e. is not the *target item*). The term is often used in the *visual search* paradigm, but is also used to describe e.g. the new items in a list of alternatives in a recog-nition task. A *token distractor* closely resembles the target, and differs only in a relatively minor detail. A *type change distractor,* on the other hand, differs in some considerable manner.

distractor task *secondary task.*

distributed memory *distributed repre-sentation.*

distributed network *distributed repre-sentation.*

distributed practice See *distribution of practice.*

distributed processing The processing of an item in sections, information from which is then integrated.

distributed representation A repre-sentation of an item which is formed by a pattern of activation across a network of units, rather than just a single unit. The latter is a *local representation.* See *parallel distributed processing.*

distribution of practice The degree to which practice at a task is spread over time. In *distributed practice*, the practice trials are spread over time, whilst in *massed practice*, they are done in one block.

distribution of practice effect The phenomenon whereby *distributed practice* tends to be more effective than *massed practice*.

divergent thinking Ability to create new ideas based upon a given topic. The term is largely interchangeable with *creativity*, and is assessed with the *creativity test*. Divergent thinking is contrasted with *convergent thinking*, which is the ability to find a single principle behind a collection of information (i.e. the former takes a single point of reference and diverges from it, whilst the latter converges several strands of thought into a single premise).

divided attention The ability to attend to and process information from more than one source simultaneously. See *divided attention costs (DACs)*. Contrast with *focused attention*.

divided attention costs (DACs) The reduction in efficiency of processing engendered by increasing the number of items which must simultaneously be attended to in a *divided attention* task.

DOCTOR *Artificial intelligence* programme whose operation is akin to that of *ELIZA*. The programme was an early attempt at generating a natural-sounding language.

doctrine of concordance The (fallacious) argument that a person's intellectual processes are in strong accordance with his/her behaviour and experience.

doctrine of formal discipline The (now largely outmoded) theory that learning certain subjects can 'discipline' the mind and enhance learning of other subjects. The converse theory is the *theory of identical elements*, which states that learning one skill will only benefit the other to the extent that they share elements in common. See *transfer of skill*.

domain (1) A situation (as in e.g. *domain-specific*). (2) A processing stage in a *mental model* (e.g. *domains of processing*).

domain-free *domain-general*.

domain-free problem See *domain-specific problem*.

domain-general See *domain-specific*.

domain-independent *domain-general*.

domain-specific Something which is only applicable to a particular situation. This contrasts with *domain-general*, which is something which applies across several situations.

domain-specific problem Problem whose solution requires specialist knowledge. This contrasts with a *domain-free problem*, which requires only general knowledge.

domains of processing *levels of processing*.

Donders' method *subtraction method*.

DRT *discrete reaction time*.

DSRT *discrete simple reaction time*.

DSST *digit-symbol substitution task*.

dual coding theory Theory that *concrete objects* are memorized in terms of their visual image and their verbal representation, and abstract items only verbally. The theory explains why *concrete images* are better recalled than abstract ones (because they are more richly represented), but it has been criticized on a number of grounds.

dual process hypothesis A (contentious) model of memory which argues that *recall* involves the retrieval of a memory trace, and then a separate verification process to ensure that it is the information being sought. *Recognition* only involves the second, verification stage, since the item is already presented for assessment.

dual process model Any model which assumes that the process being modelled consists of two stages.

dual route model Any model which assumes that the same act can be performed by two different means (see e.g. *dual route reading model*).

dual route pronunciation model Any model of pronunciation which assumes that two separate processes are used in determining how a read word should be pronounced. Typically, this assumes that there are separate processes, (i) for determining the rules of how to pronounce groups of letters within a word, and (ii) concerning the features of whole words. See *lexical analogy pronunciation model*.

dual route reading model Any model of reading which assumes that two separate processes are used in identifying words. Typically, these are methods of recognizing words by their visual appearance and by their *phonological* structure (e.g. a *visual word recognition system* and a *phonic mediation* system).

dual task method *concurrent tasks.*

dual tasks interference Interference in performing one task in a *dual task method* created by the demands of the other task being performed.

dualism See *Descartes' theory of mind.*

Duncker ray problem *ray problem.*

dustbowl empiricism Derogatory term for research which concentrates on accurately cataloguing a phenomenon without giving appropriate consideration to the work's relevance (usually, this means relevance to current theories, rather than anything so mundane as relevance to real life).

dynamic memory *Mental model* of memory which emphasizes that memory changes and constantly modifies itself – e.g. when assimilating new information, and when *schemata* 'customize' to fit each occasion.

dynamic memory span The *span* on a task in which subjects are presented with a continuous stream of items, and are asked to recall as many immediately previous items as possible when the stream unexpectedly stops.

dynamic system A system in which a change in one component affects the workings of the whole of the system.

dysgraphia A profound spelling/writing difficulty (although note there is evidence of some spelling/writing ability) which is not commensurate with the subject's intelligence, and which occurs in spite of adequate schooling. Can be innate or can result from brain damage.

dyslexia A profound reading difficulty (although note there is evidence of some reading ability) which is not commensurate with the subject's intelligence, and which occurs in spite of adequate schooling. Can be innate or can result from brain damage.

dysphasia See *aphasia.*

E

early bottleneck theories See *bottleneck theories*.

early selection theory of attention *early bottleneck theory*.

E.B. Pseudonym of the patient whose symptoms and behaviour were reported in an often-cited case study of absence of *inner speech*.

Ebbinghaus curve *forgetting curve*.

Ebbinghaus function *rate of forgetting*.

echo An item in *echoic memory*.

echoic memory A very short-term (lasting a few seconds at maximum) auditory store of just-encountered auditory information. The visual equivalent is *iconic memory*.

echoic store *echoic memory*.

ecological approach Any method or theory which emphasizes *ecological validity*.

ecological validity Term describing a study which is a realistic simulation of a real life event, and/or which tests skills used in 'real life'. This contrasts with a *laboratory study*, in which the skills tested and the test surroundings are artificial. E.g. asking subjects to remember to buy items on a trip to the supermarket might be classed as having ecological validity. Conversely, remembering a list of nonsense syllables whilst seated in a testing room would be classed as a laboratory study. See *biological plausibility*.

ecphoria Reviving a memory trace.

ecphory *ecphoria*.

EEG *electroencephalograph*.

effect, law of See *law of effect*.

effective visual field *total perceptual span*.

effort after meaning The phenomenon whereby subjects tend to distort memories to fit a pre-existing *schema*. See *War of the Ghosts*.

eidetic image *Mental imagery* which is extraordinarily vivid. Only a tiny minority of people (called *eidetikers*) experience it.

eidetiker See *eidetic image*.

Einstellung German term meaning 'set'. It denotes the set of expectations a subject forms about forthcoming stimuli, based upon prior expectations. This is a useful *heuristic*, but can lead to errors (e.g. if one's life experience of dogs has been confined to poodles, an encounter with a Irish wolfhound might be something of a surprise).

E,K,4,7 task *Wason card task*.

elaborated structure A description of a network in which the previously-stored knowledge can be used to make *elaborative inferences*.

elaborateness of processing *depth of processing*.

elaboration (memory) Enhancing the memorability of an item or set of items by 'enriching' their mental image. See *keyword technique, method of loci technique* and *peg-word system*.

elaboration coding *elaboration*.

elaborative inference *Inference* using prior knowledge to make sense of an otherwise nonsensical or ambiguous piece of information. E.g. the sentence 'she drove the Ford' is ambiguous unless one knows that 'Ford' with a capital 'F' denotes a car.

elaborative rehearsal *elaboration.*

electroencephalograph Often shortened to *EEG.* A device measuring the pattern of electrical activity (the *evoked potential (EP)*) on the scalp and by extrapolation, of the *cerebral cortex* underneath. The rate of activity and where on the scalp it occurs can give some insight into how active and healthy an individual's brain is, and which parts of the cortex are most heavily used in different mental tasks.

ELI *English Language Interpreter.*

ELINOR *LNR.*

ELIZA Computerized programme which mimics a client-centred therapist. Whatever the patient 'says' (types into the computer), Eliza replies with a comment built upon it, but without offering direct advice (essentially, the aim of the therapy is to make the patient sort out problems for him/herself). E.g.

PATIENT: 'I feel depressed'

ELIZA: 'Why do you feel depressed?'

PATIENT: 'Because of my mother'

ELIZA: 'Tell me about your mother'

etc.

Elizabeth Pseudonym of an *eidetiker* in an often-cited case study.

EM *event memory.*

emergent features Characteristics exhibited by an object which are not features of the sub-sections which make up the object.

Emperor's New Mind, The Title of a textbook by R. Penrose (mathematician), which, among discussions of physics and mathematics, argues against *strong AI*, and suggests that without a deeper and more profound knowledge of physics, we cannot fully understand the workings of the mind.

empirical Pertaining to *empiricism.*

empiricism (1) Philosophical doctrine which states that our knowledge is derived from the senses, and hence all that is learnt comes from experience (as opposed to e.g. innate beliefs which we are born possessing). The term *empiricists* refers to philosophers who adhere to this view, and particularly to the 'founding fathers' of Berkely, Hume and Locke. The school of thought is largely opposed to *rationalism.* (2) The use of experimentation and observation (e.g. in research).

empiricists See *empiricism.*

empty word A word which in the context of the sentence or phrase adds no extra information but which is necessary to make a grammatical construction (e.g. 'THERE we are, that's better isn't it?').

encoding Processing information so that it can be stored in the memory.

encoding effects *encoding specificity.*

encoding specificity The phenomenon whereby memory for items is best when the conditions and context at encoding and at retrieval are identical. For more precise definitions, see *context-dependency.*

encoding specificity principle An argument by Tulving that the probability of recalling an item is dependent on the degree of similarity between the contexts of the learning and recall sessions.

end anchoring See *linear ordering phenomenon.*

English Language Interpreter (ELI) Sub-section of the *Script Applier Mechanism*, responsible for creating *conceptual dependency* representations of text.

EP *evoked potential.*

engram (1) The neuronal state by which a memory is stored. (2) More loosely, a memory trace.

epiphenomenon A process which is a by-product of another process and in itself has no *functional significance.*

episodic memory See *semantic memory.*

epistemic awareness A person's understanding about what he or she knows (the quantity, its accuracy, etc.). Also called *metaknowledge.* Compare with *metamemory* and *systemic awareness.*

epistemology The theory and study of knowledge, and particularly of how it is acquired.

epoch (parallel distributed processing) One cycle of processing.

error signal See *feedback signal.*

equivalence (artificial intelligence/ computer simulation) *functional equivalence.*

Eureka effect *incubation effect.*

event memory (EM) *Episodic memory* of a particular type of event. A **generalized event memory (GEM)** is a memory of general features of similar events. These can be used to 'feed' a related *event schema.* See *situational memory.*

event schema (1) General knowledge about a situation being described. See *story schema.* (2) *script.*

everyday memory A general term for how memory is used in everyday life as opposed to in a *laboratory task.* See *ecological validity.*

evoked potential (EP) See *electroencephalograph.*

EVS *eye-voice span.*

excitation (1) In neurophysiology, causing a neuron to fire, or increasing the rate at which it fires. (2) By extension, in some *mental models* (and particularly in *parallel distributed processing*), causing a unit to be activated, or increasing the vigour with which it sends signals. See *inhibition.*

excitatory connection Connection in a *parallel distributed processing* model which causes *excitation.*

exemplar A concept of a typical member of a category produced from experience of the attributes of other members of that category.

exhaustive search *exhaustive serial scanning.*

exhaustive serial scanning See *serial scanning.*

expanding rehearsal Progressively increasing the interval between successive practice sessions. This is held to optimize learning, because as the subject becomes more proficient, the rate at which information is lost decreases, and therefore the subject can last longer without needing to revive memories.

experiential knowledge *experiential memory.*

experiential memory The mental storage of feelings about a piece of information (usually applied to *autobiographical memory* – e.g. how one felt about one's first day at school). Compare with *declarative knowledge/memory.*

expert memory The manner in which the memory of an expert at a task is organized for the particular task in question.

expert system *Artificial intelligence* programme which attempts to replicate the performance of a human expert at a particular task (e.g. given a set of symptoms, to diagnose an illness, such as *MYCIN*).

explicit memory Memory for specific facts. This is contrasted with *implicit memory*, which is information not stored in the form in which it is recalled, but which is calculated from explicit memory. E.g. in an often-cited example, one has explicit memories that the Statue of Liberty is in New York, and that New York is on the eastern coast of America. If asked 'which way does the Statue of Liberty face?', one can calculate that it looks eastwards, given the explicit memories.

expressive *Speech act* which serves as a conversational filler, but which may be necessary on the social level of indicating good manners (e.g. 'please', 'thank you', etc.).

expressive aphasia See *aphasia.*

extension (concept) See *intension (concept).*

external memory aid *Mnemonic* aid which acts as an environmental reminder of to-be-remembered information (e.g. a knot in the handkerchief, a diary, etc.). This contrasts with an *internal memory aid*, which is a mnemonic aid purely located in the mind (e.g. *method of loci technique*, or simply trying to remember to do something).

external speech See *inner speech.*

externally derived memories Memories of events which really occurred (in the 'external' world). Compare with *internally derived memories*, and see *reality monitoring.*

extralogical inference An inference based upon general knowledge.

extrinsic context See *intrinsic context.*

E.Y. Pseudonym of the patient whose symptoms and behaviour were reported in an often-cited case study of *blindsight.*

eye-voice span (EVS) In reading aloud, the amount of text which the eye has seen but the mouth has not yet spoken. Measured by getting subjects to read aloud, and then (without warning) taking the text away from them or otherwise blocking their view of it. To the subjects' surprise, they can usually remember the next one or two phrases beyond the phrase being read when the text was removed.

eyewitness memory The recollections of people who have witnessed an event. Usually this is a real-life crime, accident or other important incident, although the term is also extended to subjects who have watched an incident especially staged by the experimenter.

eyewitness testimony *eyewitness memory.*

F

F test (1) The assessment of whether an analysis of variance test is statistically significant. (2) A *mental rotation* test in which the subject must decide if a symbol is a rotated letter 'F' or not. (3) A *mental imagery* test in which the subject must mentally scan a letter 'F' and announce if each corner in turn points outwards or inwards.

face recognition system In a *mental model*, a stage or process responsible for recognizing faces. There is some evidence that there are specialized areas of the brain which perform just such a function.

Face Recognition Units (FRUs) See *Interactive Activation and Completion (IAC) network.*

facilitatory priming See *priming.*

faculty psychology Theory of psychology which argues that distinct areas of the brain control different psychological skills, and hence that ability at one skill is not necessarily correlated with abilities at others.

fallacy (1) An argument which is internally inconsistent. (2) A false belief (colloquial).

false alarm *false positive.*

false memory A 'memory' of an event which never occurred. May be symptomatic of a mental illness, or may be an erroneous reconstruction of faint real memories taken out of context. See *recovered memory.*

false memory syndrome See *recovered memory.*

false negative See *true positive.*

false positive See *true positive.*

false recognition *false positive.*

false syllogism A *syllogism* which produces a false statement.

false triggering *Slip of action* in which the subject begins an appropriate action at an inappropriate time.

falsifiability A concept which has gained popularity through the work of Karl Popper (twentieth century philosopher), and which argues that a theory or finding cannot satisfactorily prove anything unless it can potentially be falsified. E.g. one could make the statement that the world was spontaneously created three seconds ago. This theory cannot be disproved (since any measures one might make to 'prove' it would be part of the process of spontaneous creation). Accordingly, the theory is untestable, since it can neither be proved nor disproved. On the other hand, a theory that china vases break if dropped from 100 ft buildings onto concrete pavements could potentially be falsified – if an ample proportion of the vases bounced, then the theory would be falsified.

familiarity decision task Task in which the subject must decide if an item appears to be familiar or unfamiliar (the term usually applies to judgements of e.g. faces of famous people, rather than e.g. lists of items presented earlier in an experiment).

family resemblance The feature of a *disjunctive concept* – namely, that not all members of a category may share a feature or features in common, and yet they are all considered to be members of the same category.

Famous Names Test (FNT) A measure of *remote memory*. Subjects are presented with a list of names of people famous for brief periods of time since the 1920s, and are asked to identify those names which they can remember being in the news at some point in the past. Included in the list are some fictitious names, to prevent subjects *confabulating* and saying 'yes' to every name on the list. The test also includes a set of very famous names (Margaret Thatcher, Winston Churchill, etc.) who have been famous for appreciable periods of time. These names are always recognized by individuals with unimpaired memory, but may cause problems for some patients suffering from certain types of *amnesia* or dementia.

fan effect See *spreading activation.*

FAS test A *word fluency test* – the subject is required to produce words beginning with F, A, and S in turn.

Fast Reading Understanding and Memory Programme (FRUMP) An *artificial intelligence* programme designed to comprehend pieces of text. The programme uses *scripts.*

father and sons problem Test of problem-solving ability, which has several variants. The essential details are that a boat can carry a maximum of z pounds in weight. The father weighs z pounds, and each of his sons weighs 0.5z pounds. How can all of them cross the river using the boat?

fault tolerance The phenomenon whereby an item will be identified even though there are faults in its presentation (e.g. perceptual – part of the image is missing; or factual – the description of the item contains errors).

FB *flashbulb memory.*

FCM *feature comparison model.*

feature An attribute of an item. Usually this refers to a physical part of it, but a more abstract connotation (e.g. *semantic feature*) can also be intended. Features can be divided into *local features*, which are attributes of a parts of the item; and *global features*, which are attributes of the whole of the item.

feature abstraction theory *feature detection theory.*

feature analysis *feature detection.*

feature comparison model (FCM) A *set-theoretic model*, principally concerned with assessing whether items are members of categories, and the speed at which such assessments can be made.

feature detection theories A group of theories which argue that we perceive objects by analysing their features (e.g. the features of a chair might be legs, arms, a seat, a back, etc.), and building the features up into a coherent pattern, which is then recognized. The theories can provide a partial explanation of how we recognize items, but they cannot give a full explanation. See e.g. *top-down processing.*

feature detector Unit in a *mental model* responsible for identifying a particular feature of an item. A set of feature detectors working together can identify the total properties of an item, and it is the sum of their workings, rather than individual efforts, which enables recognition to occur. See *feature detection theories.*

feature integration Combining two or more features of a display in order to identify it.

feature integration error Error in which the incorrect features are combined to create an erroneous identification.

feature level In many models, the level (see *level (mental model)*) at which *feature detectors* operate.

feature set theory Theory that items in *semantic memory* are arranged in terms of sets of features.

feature testing Scanning an item by its individual features in an attempt to identify it.

feature theory *feature detection theory.*

feed forward lateral inhibition See *lateral inhibition.*

feedback Information given to the subject about his/her performance (through self-monitoring or provided by the experimenter). This can be provided after the subject has finished a task, or whilst s/he is still doing it. In either case, the aim is to alter the manner in which the subject subsequently performs the same task. *Positive feedback* indicates that the subject is behaving correctly, and hence encourages him/her to act in a similar manner in the future. *Negative feedback* indicates that the subject's actions are wrong or excessive, causing a diminution in their production, or the adoption of a different strategy. The mechanism by which feedback occurs is called the *feedback loop.*

feedback control *closed loop process.*

feedback loop See *feedback.*

feedback signal In some versions of *control theory*, the self-perception of performance. This is compared with a *reference signal*, which is the desired goal. A discrepancy between the feedback and reference signals creates an *error signal.* Alterations in performance seek to minimize and ultimately eliminate the error signal (i.e. to make the reference and feedback signals match).

feeling of knowing (FOK) A person's understanding of his or her own level of knowledge (i.e. how good he or she feels it is). Particularly applied to situations where a person has given a factual answer and is asked to judge how confident he or she is that it is correct. Compare with *epistemic awareness* (usually used in a more general sense). See *metamemory.*

FERMI *Artificial intelligence* problem-solving programme. Stands for 'Flexible Expert Reasoner with Multimodal Inferencing'.

filler word A word which must be in a phrase or sentence for it to be grammatically correct, but which is so familiar that the reader pays less attention to it than to other words (e.g. the words 'a' and 'be' in this sentence).

filter The mechanism by which *selective attention* selects certain stimuli for more detailed processing.

filter theory Any model of *selective attention* which argues that unattended stimuli are excluded from detailed processing.

first letter technique *initial letter priming.*

first past the post model *horse race model.*

fixation Looking at an item and processing information from it.

fixation (reading) The periods when the eye is stationary during the reading process.

fixation point In some experiments (particularly those using computer screen displays) the point where the subject is directed to look to receive the visual stimulus.

fixation position The area of an item being processed during a *fixation*.

fixed set procedure See *positive set*.

flashbulb memory (FB) The recall of an emotionally-charged event which is, subjectively, more vivid than a 'conventional' memory. The memory is unusual in that the subject remembers (often in some detail) his or her own situation when s/he heard the news – information which is often missing from conventional recollections. Typical examples are (for those old enough) remembering where one was and what one was doing when John F Kennedy was shot, or when learning that a close relative had died. It should not be supposed, however, that flashbulb memories are necessarily any more accurate in objective terms than other forms of memory. See *Piaget's 'kidnapping'*.

Flesch formula Commonly-used *readability* formula.

floor effect Effect achieved by giving a group a test which is too difficult – an undesirably large proportion of the group members scores zero or nearly zero marks, making discrimination between them impossible. See *ceiling effect*.

fluency The ease with which information can be produced.

fluent aphasia Synonym of *Wernicke's aphasia*, and more generally, of any *receptive aphasia*.

fluid intelligence The ability to solve problems for which there are no solutions derivable from formal training or cultural practices. There is usually an added assumption that to have a high level of fluid intelligence, a person must solve the said problems quickly. Fluid intelligence roughly corresponds to a layperson's concept of 'wit'.

FNT *famous names test*.

focal attentional process *attentional process*.

focal attentive process *attentional process*.

focal colour A colour which is generally agreed to be the best example of a particular colour word. By extension, a ***nonfocal colour*** is a poor example of a colour word. E.g a 'primary colour' red is a good example of 'red', whilst a 'dusty pink' colour is not.

focus gambling See *conservative focusing*.

focused attention *selective attention*.

foil *distractor*.

FOK *feeling of knowing*.

font (printing) The physical 'style' of print used. E.g. there is a clear difference between the fonts used by a printing press and a typewriter.

font face *font*.

forced choice recognition task See *recognition task*.

forgetting curve See *rate of forgetting*.

form priming See *priming*.

formal discipline *doctrine of formal discipline*.

formboard test General term for any test in which the subject is required to insert shapes into holes with the same outline in a board. The test assesses *visuo-spatial* and *psychomotor* skills.

forward masking See *masking*.

forward memory search In searching through one's (usually *autobiographical*) memories, starting with the earliest memories and searching chronologically forwards. Compare with *backward memory search*.

forward telescoping The tendency to think that an event occurred more recently than it really did (particularly applies to famous events).

four card problem *Wason card task.*

fovea The site on the retina at which light from the lens of the eye is focused. It contains the highest concentration of receptor cells, and is the area with the highest visual acuity. Accordingly, *foveal vision* is the most detailed people have. The area surrounding the fovea (the *parafovea*) has fewer receptors, and accordingly has poorer acuity. Accordingly, *parafoveal vision* tends to be poorer, and stimuli within this region stand a higher probability of being unnoticed.

foveal vision See *fovea.*

foxes and geese problem See *river crossing problem.*

frame A *schema* for an object or a particular scene. Compare with *script.*

framing The degree to which a *frame* shapes the processing/memory of an event/item.

free morpheme *Morpheme* which is itself a word.

free recall A memory task in which items may be recalled in any order (i.e. the order in which they were originally presented does not have to be reproduced). Compare with *serial recall.*

frequency (words) The frequency with which a particular word occurs in conventional usage. **High frequency words** (e.g. 'and', 'see', etc.) occur often, and **low frequency words** (e.g. 'aardvark', 'paradigm', etc.) occur very rarely. Word frequency can affect aspects of performance, such as the speed with which they are recognized, their memorability, etc.

frequency judgement task A memory task in which the subject must judge how often a particular item or set of items appear in a presentation.

frequency paradox The phenomenon whereby *high frequency words* are better *recalled* but less well *recognized* than *low frequency words.*

fricative (phonetics) Pertaining to a *phone* whose production involves a constriction in part of the vocal tract (causing friction – hence the name). A useful rule of thumb is that the same fricative consonant can be produced for as long as the speaker has breath to do it.

front anchoring See *linear ordering phenomenon.*

frontal lobes The front section of the *cerebral cortex* extending back to the temples. Primarily involved in planning and controlling actions and thoughts (e.g. getting words in the right order when speaking, producing socially appropriate behaviour).

FRU *Face Recognition Unit.*

FRUMP *Fast Reading Understanding and Memory Programme.*

function word substitution Reading error in which a *function word* is misread as another function word (e.g. 'the' is read as 'an').

function words Words whose primary purpose is to provide *syntax* rather than meaning (e.g. 'and', 'but', 'by', etc.). See *content words.*

functional architecture See *cognitive penetrability.*

functional asymmetry *lateralization.*

functional equivalence The degree to which two items resemble each other in performance. In *artificial intelligence/computer simulation*, there must be some level of functioning at which the computer programme's performance resembles that of the human mind it is imitating for the exercise to be worthwhile. Typically (although not invariably), equivalence is primarily judged in terms of the responses which the computer gives in a given situation which are compared to those of a human subject under the same conditions. A programme that mimicked human performance might be said to be functionally equivalent. However, researchers are usually also interested in how the result was achieved. If the programme strongly resembles the processing stages hypothesized to take place in the human mind, then it is said to have *strong equivalence*. Conversely, if the programme does not resemble human processing, then it is said to have *weak equivalence*. Tangential to this, a programme which only mimics one specific aspect of human performance is said to have *specific equivalence*, whilst a more general resemblance is said to show *general equivalence*.

functional fixedness Term devised by Duncker to denote a failure to see a novel use for an object because knowledge of its conventional uses dominates in the subject's thoughts. E.g. in the *candle problem*, the subject is presented with a candle, some matches, and a box of drawing pins (thumbtacks). The subject is told to attach the candle to the wall and light it. The solution is to empty the box, pin it to the wall, and place the candle on the box before lighting it. Many subjects could not do the task because, it was argued, they could only see the box as a container. In the *two string problem*, the subject is presented with two pieces of string suspended from the ceiling, with the instruction that they are to be tied together. The two pieces are sufficiently far apart that the subject cannot reach them simultaneously. The subject is provided with a variety of tools, including a pair of pliers.

The solution to the problem is to tie the pliers to one of the pieces of string, to create a pendulum. This enables the subject to swing one piece of string so that it can be caught whilst holding the other piece of string.

functional fixity *functional fixedness.*

functional inference *Inference* that a particular event has occurred as the consequence of a particular action.

functional knowledge *procedural knowledge.*

functional level In a communication, the level of interpretation at which the grammatical structure of the message is processed.

functional literacy The basic level of reading skills required for a particular occupation or lifestyle. E.g., for most unskilled jobs, a reading age of 11 is the maximum required. See *functional reading.*

functional reading The ability to read basic instructional materials at the barest level of proficiency expected by the society in which the subject is living. See *functional literacy.*

functional significance The use of something, aside from its simple existence. The term is used in the debate over the *analogue representation* theory of visual imagery by those who argue that the mental picture of a visual image serves no functional purpose, but is a by-product of the 'real' processing.

functional symmetry See *lateralization.*

fusion In perception, combining information from different sources to create a single image.

fuzzy borders See *fuzzy sets.*

fuzzy concept *fuzzy set.*

fuzzy knowledge Knowledge which is not precise (as in *absolute knowledge*) but which can be generalized to a wide range of situations with reasonable (if not total) accuracy. Also, any knowledge which requires probabilistic judgements (e.g. which team will win the league championship).

fuzzy sets Sets whose boundaries are indistinct (*fuzzy borders*), and hence where it is difficult to decide if some items merit inclusion in a particular set (e.g. shades of a red – when is a colour classified as red and when is it classified as orange?).

G

g General intellectual capacity – a term devised by Charles Spearman (early twentieth century) to describe an ability he felt underpinned all intellectual skills. Today often used more loosely to denote subjects' general level of intelligence. See *G*.

G *g*.

Galton cueing technique *Cued recall* technique in which the subject is prompted to recall an *autobiographical memory* which is associated with a word provided by the experimenter (e.g. Experimenter: 'Jam'; Subject: 'I remember making jam with my mother in the summer of 1946').

gambler's fallacy The mistaken belief that because there has been a long string of one type of *mutually exclusive event*, another type of event 'must' occur soon. E.g. because there have been ten 'heads' tossed in a row, 'tails' must come up next. This is fallacious, because on each toss of the coin, the odds of 'heads' and 'tails' are even – the coin is not influenced by what has gone before. The debunking of the gambler's fallacy often leaves people with the equally erroneous impression that a long sequence of one type of event (e.g. tossing 'heads' ten times in a row) is not unusual; it is unusual, in that a mixture of heads and tails is far more probable. This does not contradict the argument that 'tails' can just as easily be thrown after a sequence of TTTTTTTTTT as after HTTHTTHTHH.

game theory The study of games and competitions by mathematical means. Often, this involves calculating the permutations of 'payoffs' which players will receive depending upon each other's actions.

garden path sentence Sentence whose meaning switches from the one which the subject initially interpreted, to a different meaning (e.g. 'Mary came bouncing down the stairs, and John sent for the doctor').

gaze contingent technique *Moving window technique* (definition 3).

gaze duration The total time spent looking at a particular part of a display.

G.B. Pseudonym of the patient in an often-cited case study, who lacked any capacity for producing speech. However, he demonstrated the effects akin to those of subjects capable of *subvocal rehearsal* in memory tests.

G.B.L. Pseudonym of the patient whose symptoms and behaviour were reported in an often-cited case study of *prosapagnosia*.

gc/Gc Symbol for *crystallized intelligence*.

gedanken experiment A study in which the experimenter thinks about the likely results of an experiment without actually running it.

GEM *generalized event memory*.

general equivalence See *functional equivalence*.

general intelligence *g*.

general mechanism (phonetics) T h e theory that perception of speech and non-speech sounds is governed by the same general process.

General Problem Solver (GPS) Computerized problem-solving programme. Uses *means-ends analysis.*

general working memory (WMG) See *working memory.*

generalization (-isation) hierarchy In a *schema* representation, the storage of information pertaining to all members of a set is not stored separately by each member of a set, but by an overarching schema representing the general attributes of the set. E.g. information on the attributes of dogs would not be kept in a poodle schema, but in a dog schema. Similarly, information on the attributes of mammals is not kept in a dog schema, but in a mammals schema. This hierarchical organization saves considerably on storage capacity, and should aid classification, by providing a ready-made taxonomic structure.

generalized event memory (GEM) See *event memory.*

generalized programme General set of instructions determining the basic parameters of a set of related acts/behaviours.

generate and recognize model A n y model of memory retrieval which argues that a set of likely answers is generated, and the most plausible candidate is then chosen from this set.

generate-test model Model of problem solving in which it is proposed that the subject generates a possible solution and then tests its efficacy.

generation effect The p h e n o m e n o n whereby items which the subject has had first to generate for him/herself (e.g. as in the *stem completion task*) are usually more likely to be remembered

than items which s/he has passively encountered.

generation-recognition model *semantic network.*

generation-recognition model (memory) Theory which states that in retrieving a memory, a number of possible responses are generated and then one is picked from this list.

generative rules *rewrite rules.*

generic memory Memories for the same event experienced on many occasions (often autobiographical – e.g. playtime at school) which have coalesced into a single stereotypical memory. Usually, memories of specific individual experiences of the event are lost. Compare with *specific memory.*

Gestalt psychology School of psychological thought (founded at the turn of the twentieth century) originally primarily concerned with perception, although more recently centred on therapeutic techniques. It argued that there is a predisposition to see the whole of an object, rather than its constituent parts. E.g. the row of dots

....

looks like a row: there is an apparent irresistible urge to see a row rather than its features. The theory is also concerned with problem solving, and emphasizes how successful solutions involve perceiving the whole of a problem, and breaking free from stereotyped views, such as *functional fixedness.*

Gf/gf Symbol for *fluid intelligence.*

Gibson's theory of direct perception Theory proposed by James Gibson (1904–1980) and subsequently developed by his wife Eleanor. Gibson argued that one perceives the world directly, without cognitive processing or the need for interpretation. For example, this can be done by identifying features of a display which are *invariants*, and remain constant in appearance. Again, Gibson argued that objects are perceived in terms of their use (*affordances*). Other, less controversial cues include *optic flow patterns* (the phenomenon whereby when moving, nearby objects appear to move past one faster than distant objects); and *texture gradients* (the phenomenon whereby nearby objects can be seen in greater detail than distant ones). The theory has been heavily criticized.

given information (linguistics) See *given-new contract.*

given-new contract The linguistic principle that a comprehensible statement should give the information necessary to 'set the scene' before providing *new information*, which can only be comprehended if the listener already possesses the *given information*. E.g. consider the statement 'You know Dave Smith? I gave him your keys.' The listener will not know who has his/her keys without the given information of the first part of the statement.

G.L. Pseudonym of the patient whose symptoms and behaviour were reported in an often-cited case study of visual *agnosia.*

global (problem solving) See *local (problem solving).*

global aphasia See *aphasia.*

global feature See *feature.*

global structure (1) The degree to which a piece of communication makes sense when considered overall. (2) Overall structure or appearance.

glottal (phonetics) Pertaining to a *phone* whose production involves the constriction of the glottis (part of the throat).

glottal stop (phonetics) Pertaining to a *phone* whose production involves the closing of the glottis (part of the throat), followed by its release. Most often heard when a vowel follows another in a word, and the two vowels must be pronounced separately.

go–no-go task *Simple reaction time* task in which the subject has only one button to press (or another single response to make).

goal The target/end result of an action and, by implication, something which is desired.

goal-directed production A *production* which is engaged in *goal directed* behaviour.

goal directedness The direction of behaviour towards a particular *goal.* The term is occasionally used of problem-solving activity.

goal knowledge state *goal state (problem solving).*

goal state (problem solving) See *problem space.*

goal switches Types of *slips of action* where a person starts on one activity, and then switches to another, either through distraction (e.g. going shopping for a newspaper and buying a bar of chocolate instead), or because of a similar and more frequently used action takes over (e.g. an habitual coffee drinker sets off to make tea and makes coffee). See also *data-driven error.*

Gollin Incomplete Figures A test of memory/*visuo-spatial* skills. The subject is shown an incomplete line drawing of a figure, and then gradually more complete drawings of the same object, until s/he can identify it. The subject is shown the figures on subsequent occasions, and the process is repeated. With the repeated exposures, the subject should require progressively fewer complete drawings before s/he successfully identifies the object.

Gottschaldt figures Simple figures embedded in more complex figures. Used in tests of *visuo-spatial* ability – the subject must locate the simple figures.

GPC rules *grapheme-phoneme correspondence rules.*

GPS *General Problem Solver.*

G.R. Pseudonym of a patient whose symptoms and behaviour were reported in an often-cited case study of *deep dysgraphia.*

graceful degradation See *parallel distributed processing.*

graded structure A structure which can be arranged in a hierarchy. The term is often used for a hierarchy of *prototypicality.*

gradient descent (parallel distributed processing) The aim of a developing *neural net* is usually to reduce error (typically, between its current and its goal state, as in e.g. *backward propagation*). Programmes are designed to reduce this error over successive *epochs* – a process called gradient descent. The process can become stuck in **local minima**. In some instances, the process may, after a period of successive reductions in errors, suddenly produce an increase in errors when further adjustment is made. It is possible that this indicates that the goal has been reached (i.e. the net has reached the best representation it can make), or it could be a temporary setback (a local minima) and a bigger change will yield further falls in the error rate. The situation is often likened to rolling a ball

down a hill – a trough in the side of the hill might trap the ball, preventing it from rolling to the bottom.

gradient of knowing *knowledge gradient.*

grain size (mental imagery) The degree of resolution of a *mental image* (i.e. the level of detail which the subject can report).

grammatical word *function word.*

grapheme The smallest written symbol whose substitution or removal changes meaning. This means that most graphemes are letters (and many commentators treat 'letter' and 'grapheme' as synonymous), but punctuation marks and commonly-accepted symbols (e.g. '@', '£', etc.) are also included in a rigid definition.

grapheme-phoneme conversion Calculating what letters sound like, and by extrapolation, what the words made from the letters sound like. An essential part of *phonic mediation.*

grapheme-phoneme correspondence (GPC) rules The rules governing *grapheme-phoneme conversion.*

graphemic Pertaining to *graphemes.*

graphemic buffer A temporary memory store used in spelling to 'hold' the memory trace of the word to be spelt while it is written. Compare with *phonemic buffer.*

graphemic output lexicon *Mental lexicon* which stores memories of how to produce written letters and letter combinations.

graphemic word production system *graphemic output lexicon.*

Gricean maxims Named after their inventor, Grice (philosopher). Following the *cooperative principle*, participants in conversations follow four maxims: quality (the speaker should be truthful);

quantity (the speaker should be succinct); relation (the speaker should stick to the point of discussion, and the listener will assume that any utterance is relevant); and manner (the speech should be unambiguous and follow a logical sequence). Particularly because of the 'relation' maxim, the listener is capable of interpreting apparently oblique statements for their underlying intent (see *pragmatics* and *speech act*).

H

H *information.*

H-testing *hypothesis testing.*

habituation The cessation of responding or reduction in response strength to a stimulus which has been presented frequently in the past.

HAM *Human Associative Memory.*

handedness The degree to which a subject prefers using one hand rather than the other (e.g. for writing, throwing, etc.). The number of 'natural' left handers is greater than the number of adults who are left-handed, because many children are encouraged/forced to be right-handed to fit in with the majority. Handedness is a far from infallible indicator of *lateralization.*

hardware An image taken from computing, denoting the relatively unchangeable aspects of mental processing (i.e. the physical structure and natural limitations of the brain). This is contrasted with *software*, which is the 'programmes' run by the hardware (i.e. psychological processes).

HARPY An *artificial intelligence* programme for speech recognition.

head morpheme *root morpheme.*

HEARSAY An *artificial intelligence* programme for speech recognition. Uses a *blackboard* process.

Hebb rule Type of *Hebbian rule. Weights* are adjusted, and the connection between two items strengthened whenever both are simultaneously active.

Hebbian net *Neural net* which functions using *Hebbian rules.*

Hebbian rules General term given to rules used in *parallel distributed processing* to adjust *weights* of connections between units. The rules have the general purpose of 'pushing' the relationship in the direction (i.e. excitatory, inhibitory or neutral) which is required for the desired overall pattern of activation within the *neural net* to be reached. Note that the rules do not have a 'conscious' goal (i.e. they are not acting like a *homunculus*). Space does not permit a full explanation of how this is accomplished. However, a flavour of the ideas can be gained by looking at some examples of Hebbian rules, such as the *Hopfield rule*, and the *Stent-Singer rule.*

hedges (psycholinguistics) Spoken expressions which indicate 'hedging one's bets' – i.e. as if the speaker is shying away from making a definitive statement (e.g. 'I guess', 'probably', etc.).

hemispheres (cortex) The *cerebral cortex* is divided into two equally sized halves along a vertical axis running from the front to the back of the head. These two halves are known as the hemispheres, and logically enough, are called the right hemisphere and the left hemisphere ('right' refers to the side one would call one's own 'right' side). In most individuals, the left hemisphere is principally responsible for linguistic skills and the right for visuo-spatial (although in some individuals, particularly left-handers, this is reversed and other, rarer, people have no simple left-right distinction). The hemispheres are linked by several pathways, of which the most important is the *corpus callosum.*

hemispheric differences Differences between the functioning of the right and left *hemispheres.*

heterarchical model Model of processing in which there is a considerable degree of interaction between different processing stages.

heterophonic homograph
See *homograph.*

heuristic A problem-solving method, which is highly likely (although not invariably) to yield the correct solution, or at least to put the subject within easy 'striking distance' of finding the correct answer. E.g. treating pi as $2\frac{2}{7}$ is a useful heuristic where a reasonably accurate but not perfect answer is required to solve e.g. the calculation of a circumference. The method is less accurate than an *algorithm,* but it may be less time consuming, and the answer may be within acceptable bounds of error. When it is not, then it is known as an *heuristic inadequacy error.*

heuristic-analytic model Model of problem-solving in which *heuristics* generate 'rough solutions' which are then analysed and sharpened into acceptably accurate answers.

heuristic inadequacy error See *heuristic.*

Hick-Hyman law *Hick's law.*

Hick's law Law which states that as the amount of *information* in a *choice reaction time* task increases, so does the reaction time.

hidden layers See *hidden units.*

hidden units In *parallel distributed processing,* any units which are not involved in receiving input or producing output. In some models, the units are conceived of existing in layers (***hidden layers***), often

with a hierarchical order (i.e. information is passed from one layer to the next as a signal is processed from input through to output).

hierarchical model Model of mental processing in which some processing units are subservient to others.

high association See *association.*

high density neighbourhood See *neighbours.*

high frequency words
See *frequency (words).*

high level process See *low level process.*

high level proposition *macroproposition.*

high level schema See *schema theory.*

high level unit Unit used in a *high level process.*

high level vocabulary Jargon. The term usually refers to the use of jargon which acts as convenient conceptual 'short-hand'.

higher level process *high level process.*

hippocampus *Sub-cortical* section of the brain whose principal function is probably in memory, and particularly in transferring information from *short-* to *long-term memory.* Damage to the hippocampus leads to an extremely debilitating *amnesia,* with patients unable to remember practically any new information.

hit *true positive.*

H.M. Famous neuropsychological patient who suffered very extensive *anterograde amnesia* following a brain operation in 1953 which was intended to cure his epileptic seizures. The operation severed the *temporal lobes* and part of the *hippocampus.*

Hoffding step The process of perceiving a sensory stimulation. The term is drawn from *Gestalt* theory.

holding capacity *memory capacity.*

holistic processing *wholistic processing.*

homograph A word which has the same spelling as another but has a different meaning and possibly a different pronunciation (e.g. 'bass'). The term *lexical ambiguity* is sometimes used to describe this. Where there is a different pronunciation and meaning, the term *heterophonic homograph* has been coined. Compare with *homonym* and *homophone.*

homomorph A representation of a set of items by a smaller set of concepts, in which many items are represented by the same concept (e.g. a homomorph of mammals might have one concept for all types of dogs).

homonym A word with the same spelling and/or sound as another word, but with different meanings (e.g. 'bank', 'there'/'their'). See *homograph* and *homophone.*

homophone A word which when pronounced, sounds the same as a word with a different spelling (e.g. 'key' and 'quay'). Compare with *homonym* and *paronym.*

homophonic error Misperceiving a word as its *homophone* (e.g. reading 'two' as 'to').

homunculus (1) A hypothesized 'little person' who sits in the head and reads and interprets the output from the brain. This is clearly nonsensical, and is advanced as a criticism of some *mental models*, which show how information can be processed, but give no satisfactory indication of what controls the running of the process, or how the end product is rendered into a form of which the mind can be consciously aware. There often appears to be a tacit assumption that the homunculus is there to steer the process, and to interpret the output (presumably whispering the answer into the subject's ear). Taking the argument further, one then has the problem of how the homunculus interprets information – is there a homunculus inside the homunculus' head (and so on, reductio ad absurdum)? (2) The representation of the body in the *cortex* – parts with greater sensitivity (e.g. hands, mouth, genitalia) are cortically represented in greater proportion than their physical size.

Hopfield rule Type of *Hebbian rule. Weights* are adjusted, and the connection between two items strengthened whenever both are simultaneously active or inactive. When one is active and the other is not, then the connection is weakened.

horse dealing problem A measure of problem-solving ability. The subject is told that a person bought a horse for e.g. £10 and sold it for £20, then subsequently bought it again for £40 and sold it for £50. How much money did s/he make or lose? The proportion of correct answers can be varied by altering the wording of the problem (e.g. if instead of saying that the person rebought the original horse, s/he buys another horse for £40, then the number of correct answers increases).

horse race model Any model of processing in which it is assumed that two or more different processes will be run in parallel in an attempt to identify the same item. Either (i) the item is given the identity created by the first process to finish the task, or (ii) the item is given the identity created by the process which accrued the largest amount of information about the item.

Human Associative Memory (HAM) A *propositional network* which analyses the form of the associations between words in sentences.

Humphrey's law Law which states that performance of an *automatic* task will worsen if the subject attempts consciously to monitor it.

hyperlexia (1) Reading accurately but with no evidence of comprehension of what is being read. See *demented dyslexia*. (2) Reading at a precociously early age.

hypothesis testing (H testing) Collecting and/or assessing information to see if it confirms or denies a hypothesis. The phrase is often used to denote *concept formation* and problem-solving strategies of this kind.

I

IAC network *Interactive Activation and Completion (IAC) network.*

ICM *instance comparison model.*

icon A very short-term (lasting less than 0.5 seconds) visual memory which is an almost literal representation of an image just seen.

iconic memory The *mnemonic* process of creating and storing *icons*. The auditory equivalent is *echoic memory.*

ideal viewing position (reading) *convenient viewing location (reading).*

identical elements theory *theory of identical elements.*

identification See *recognition.*

idiolect An individual's language use (particularly its idiosyncrasies).

IHTT *interhemispheric transmission time.*

ill defined problem Problem in which the *initial state* and the *goal state* are badly defined. See *well defined problem.*

illegal error *violation error.*

illegal word A *nonsense word* which uses letter combinations which are not found in real words (e.g. 'sgrfdw'). By extension, a *legal word* is a one which uses conventional spelling patterns (e.g. 'floddlepop').

illocutionary force The intent of a statement, which may be at odds with its literal meaning (e.g. 'would you like to wash your hands?').

illusory conjunction An inaccurate blending of features from separate items (e.g. *migration error*).

image scanning Scanning a *mental image* to examine its details. Generally, it takes longer to 'move' from one part of the image to another the longer the physical distance between the parts in the physical counterpart of the mental image. E.g. in a mental image of a map of the British Isles, it might take longer to 'move' from London to Edinburgh than it would to move from London to Cambridge.

imageability How easily a *mental image* of an item can be created (usually, the higher the imageability, the better remembered the item is).

imageless thought Thought process which produces no *mental imagery.*

imagen In some models of mental functioning, a unit representing *visuo-spatial* items. See *logogen.*

imagery *mental imagery.*

imagist argument *analogue representation.*

immediacy assumption (reading) (1) The assumption that, as soon as the reader encounters a word, s/he immediately attempts to process it. (2) The hypothesis that a word is processed to the point of comprehension before the next word is fixated upon.

immediate memory *short-term memory.*

impenetrable system *opaque system.*

implicit learning *implicit memory.*

implicit memory (1) See *explicit memory.* (2) Knowledge about something of which one has no conscious recollection of having studied.

implicit speech *inner speech.*

incidental learning Information which has been acquired without conscious intent. E.g. in watching the television it is possible to learn a vast amount of trivial knowledge without ever explicitly intending to do so. This contrasts with *intentional learning*, in which the subject has a deliberate plan to learn a particular body of knowledge.

incongruent priming See *priming*.

inconsistent analogy (spelling) See *pronunciation by analogy*.

inconsistent words See *consistency (spelling)*.

incubation effect Phenomenon whereby a subject can work at a problem without success for a long time, and then find that the answer 'pops into' his/her mind unbidden.

independent context memory See *context memory*.

independent tasks Tasks which can be performed concurrently without interfering with each other.

indirect directive *Directive* which can only be complied with if the listener comprehends its *pragmatics* rather than its literal meaning (e.g. 'would you like to wash your hands?').

indirect recall/recognition See *direct recall/recognition*.

individual differences The study of how and why people differ psychologically (particularly in intelligence and personality).

induction *inductive reasoning*.

inductive inference *inductive reasoning*.

inductive reasoning See *deductive reasoning*.

infantile amnesia *childhood amnesia*.

inference Extrapolating from existing knowledge to form new pieces of knowledge. See *analogical inference, bridging inference, causal inference, deductive inference, elaborative inference, functional inference, inductive inference, instrumental inference, logical inference, metamemory inference, spatial inference* and *temporal inference*. See also *schema*.

inference engine Segment of an *artificial intelligence* programme responsible for making *inferences*.

inferential intrusion error An *intrusion error* which is created by drawing assumptions from a *schema* appropriate to the to-be-remembered item or event. E.g. erroneously recalling 'confetti' as being part of a list of to-be-remembered words about weddings.

inferred number right (INR) score Traditional scoring system for a multiple choice test, in which the first answer given is the only one accepted. See *answer until correct (AUC) score*.

information (H) (1) As used in many *information processing* theories, the term refers to the number of *bits* a stimulus can be divided into. A bit is a set of two equally likely alternatives. (For the mathematically-minded, this means that the number of bits $= \log 2N$, where N is the number of choices.) Where outcomes are not equally likely, formulae are available to calculate the number of bits. (2) The term is also widely used in the lay sense of the word.

information channels The concept that at any one time, the mind can usually select from several channels of information (e.g. from input from surroundings, trains of thought originating from within, etc.).

information processing An explanation of cognitive functioning in terms borrowed from computer programming. There are many variants, but essentially, the processing of a piece of information is seen in terms of a sequence of mechanisms, each of which manipulates the information so that it is 'readable' by the next process in the chain (often collectively called *processing stages*). E.g. in learning something, there will be processes for handling the initial perception of the images (***input processes***); further processes for formatting the information so that it can be stored (***storage processes***); and yet further processes for retrieving this information when it needs to be recalled (***output processes***). See *information*.

information processing system (IPS) System of mental functioning couched in terms of *information processing*.

information theory Branch of communication sciences concerned with the transmission and reception of knowledge in abstract, logical forms. It provides the basis for the *information processing* approach to cognition.

inhibition (1) In neurophysiology, preventing a neuron from firing, or suppressing the rate at which it fires. (2) By extension, in some *mental models* (and particularly in *parallel distributed processing*), preventing a unit from being activated, or reducing the vigour with which it sends signals. See *excitation*.

inhibitory connection Connection in a *parallel distributed processing* model which causes *inhibition*.

initial knowledge state *initial state (problem solving)*.

initial letter priming Providing subjects with the initial letters of words in a list the subject is trying to recall.

initial state (problem solving) See *problem space*.

inner speech The inner thoughts – e.g. internal monologues, or the 'voice in the head' which most people experience when reading. This contrasts with ***external speech***, which is speech for communicating with other people.

input lexicon Any *mental lexicon* responsible for comprehending input (particularly speech and print).

input modality The format in which the stimuli are presented to the subject (e.g. whether they are auditory or visual).

input processes See *information processing*.

INR score *inferred number right score*.

inside-outside processing *top-down processing*.

inspection time (IT) The length of time for which a stimulus must be presented before the subject correctly recognizes it on a particular percentage of occasions (the percentage figure is determined by the experimenter).

instance comparison model (ICM) Model of *concept formation*. Argues that subjects learn concepts not by detailed analysis of features, but by classifying items according to which previously encountered items they most resemble, and assigning them to the same category.

instrumental case See *case grammar*.

instrumental inference *Inference* that a particular instrument was used to perform a deed, even though it is not explicitly stated (e.g. 'a man was shot' – one infers that a gun was used).

integral attribute Feature of an item which cannot be mentally separated from other features (e.g. the flavourings in many soft drinks, such as Coca Cola, etc.). This contrasts with a ***separable attribute***, in which the feature can be regarded separately (e.g. height can often be perceived as a distinct feature of an object).

integrated partial parsing (IPP) *Artificial intelligence* text comprehension programme. The programme uses *MOPS*.

integrative visual buffer A *buffer* which assembles an overall 'picture' from the information gained from individual fixations on a display.

intellectualization (-isation) (1) Talking about a problem as a means of avoiding tackling it. (2) Treating a problem in a detached manner as an intellectual puzzle.

intelligence The level of ease with which a subject can accurately respond to intellectual tasks. Since the range of tasks which have an intellectual component is vast, it is unlikely that precisely the same skill underlies all of them. Equally, it is unlikely that a different type of intelligence is required for each and every different task. However, researchers have made claims for both these extremes and practically every permutation in between. See *fluid intelligence* and *crystallized intelligence*.

intelligence quotient (IQ) Often (erroneously) used as a synonym for *intelligence*. The intelligence quotient is used to denote how intelligent a person is, in comparison with the rest of his or her age group. Traditionally, a score of 100 has denoted a person of average intelligence for his/her age cohort – i.e. 50% of the group are more clever, 50% are less clever then this person. A score of more than 130 indicates someone who is exceptionally bright for the group (i.e. there are few people in the age group with better scores) and a score of 70 or below indicates someone who is unusually ungifted.

intelligence test Any test which claims to measure *intelligence*. Typically, the test will yield a single measure of *general intelligence*, which is usually expressed in terms of an *IQ* score.

intension (concept) The properties of a concept which define its membership (e.g. the intension of the concept 'dog' might include 'has fur', 'has four legs', etc.). This contrasts with the **extension** of a concept, which is all the members of a concept (e.g. poodles, Shetland sheepdogs, etc.).

intentional learning See *incidental learning*.

intentional memory Memory of plans and sequences necessary to enact a particular plan.

inter-stimulus interval (ISI) The gap between the presentation of one item and the next. This can be important in determining how the items are processed, both qualitatively and quantitatively (e.g. see *Posner letter matching task*).

inter-trial interval (ITI) The gap between the end of one test and the start of the next.

interactive activation Term used by McClelland to describe his *interactive model* of language processing.

Interactive Activation and Completion (IAC) network Model of face recognition by Burton, Bruce and Johnston, which contains three processes: *Face Recognition Units (FRUs)* which identify the physical features; *Person Identity Nodes (PINs)* which identify names for the faces; and *Semantic Information Units (SIUs)* which identify information about the person's attributes (occupation, nationality, etc.).

interactive context memory See *context memory*.

interactive model Any model which stresses the interaction between different sub-processes. I.e. a mixture of *top-down* and *bottom-up* processes.

interference The reduction in performance on one task caused by another. Most commonly used to describe how a set of memories interferes with memory for another set; how being forced to hear or see stimuli other than the *target* interferes with processing of the target; and how being required to perform more than one task simultaneously affects their execution. Contrast with *decay*.

interference theory of forgetting See *trace decay theory of forgetting*.

interhemispheric transmission time (IHTT) The time taken for a nervous impulse to pass from one *hemisphere* to the other.

interlingua A mediating language required to translate from one symbolic representation to another.

intermediate states (problem solving) See *problem space*.

intermodal *cross-modal*.

internal memory aid See *external memory aid*.

internal psychophysics The study of *mental imagery*.

internally derived memories Memories of schemes and actions which have only ever been thought of, and which have never occurred in reality (i.e. memories of events from the 'internal' world). Compare with *externally derived memories*, and see *reality monitoring*.

International Phonetic Alphabet (IPA) Standardized alphabet of characters representing all the *phonemes* used in human languages.

interpolated task A task inserted between two others, usually with the intention of distracting the subject from what has been and what is to come (e.g. between learning a list of words and recalling them).

intersection search In a *network model* (e.g. *semantic network*) – sending signals from two or more *nodes* along their communication links with other nodes to see if the signals meet. If they do, then a connection between the nodes can be judged to exist.

interval of uncertainty See *threshold*.

intrinsic context Properties peculiar to an item itself. This contrasts with **extrinsic context**, which refers to the properties of the environment in which an item is encountered.

introspection The process of examining one's own thoughts. Common research tool of early psychologists, and heavily criticized by the *behaviourists*. It has had something of a revival in recent years, since introspection can reveal much about *mental imagery*.

intrusion error (1) In memory tasks, 'recalling' an item which was not present. (2) In reading, inserting a word which is not in the to-be-read material. (3) In *selective attention* tasks, reporting information which is part of the *unattended message*.

intuition Selecting a solution and/or interpretation which cannot be supported by rigid, formal logic, but which accords with a subjective feeling that it is correct. See *belief bias* and *pragmatic reasoning*.

invariances *invariants*.

invariant features *invariants*.

invariants See *Gibson's theory of direct perception*.

inverted U curve A curve which looks like an upside-down U-shape. Often cited in conjunction with *Yerkes-Dodson law*.

involuntary memory (1) The spontaneous and entirely unbidden recollection of a past event, often with some emotional feelings. The 'bliss of solitude' according to Wordsworth. (2) The recall of an unbidden memory which is connected with what one is currently perceiving, or is connected with a memory one has deliberately recalled (e.g. in recalling one's address, a mental image of one's house might appear).

IPA *International Phonetic Alphabet.*

IPP *integrated partial parsing.*

IPS *information processing system.*

IQ *intelligence quotient.*

irregular spelling See *regular spelling.*

irregular word Word with an *irregular spelling.*

irrelevant speech effect *unattended speech effect.*

ISI *inter-stimulus interval.*

isomorphism (1) Identical basic structures. (2) The belief that neurological structure mimics the structure of the 'real-life' items being imagined/perceived. The concept is in most instances an illogical one, but the 'milder' phrase, *second order isomorphism*, is sometimes used to describe *analogue representation.*

IT *inspection time.*

ITI *inter-trial interval.*

J

jargon aphasia Syntactically garbled speech (often containing *paraphasias* and neologisms) which is characteristic of many *aphasias*.

J.B.R. Neurological patient in an often-cited case study, with the remarkable deficit of being unable to define animate objects, although descriptions of inanimate objects were accurate.

J.C. (1) Neuropsychological patient in an often-cited case study, who suffered from *surface dyslexia*. (2) Different patient suffering from *deep dysgraphia*.

J.C.U. Pseudonym of a patient whose symptoms and behaviour were reported in an often-cited case study of *anomia*.

JND *just noticeable difference.*

JNND *just not noticeable difference.*

John Dean's memory Famous study of *everyday memory* by Ulric Neisser on John Dean, one of President Nixon's aides. Dean described his conversations with Nixon to the Watergate Committee. They were subsequently checked by Neisser against the tapes made by Nixon (unknown to Dean) of the same conversations. Neisser found that although Dean was drastically wrong about many details, the overall themes of what he said occurred were accurate.

Julesz random dot stereogram *random dot stereogram.*

just not noticeable difference (JNND) See *threshold.*

just noticeable difference (JND) See *threshold.*

K

K-line *knowledge-line.*

kana See *kanji.*

kanji *Logographic* writing system, which, used in partnership with **kana**, a *syllabic writing system*, forms the Japanese writing system.

keyword technique *Mnemonic* technique in which the subject learns to associate two items by forming a striking visual image which links them. E.g. in learning to associate the words 'banana' and 'car', the subject might form an image of a giant banana driving a car. See *method of loci technique* and *peg-word system.*

K.F. Neurological patient in an often-cited study, with a preserved *long-term memory*, but a severely deteriorated *short-term memory.*

K.J. Pseudonym of a patient whose symptoms and behaviour were reported in an often-cited case study of *amnestic syndrome.*

knowledge and true belief Philosophical problem involving the distinction between one's knowledge and what would constitute a true belief, and whether there is a cognitive basis for the distinction.

knowledge base In *artificial intelligence,* the level and amount of appropriate knowledge the programme possesses about a particular situation.

knowledge based system *expert system.*

knowledge gradient In some *feeling of knowing* studies, the subjects are given a multiple choice general knowledge test, and asked to grade how confident they are that their answers are correct. Usually, the more confident the subjects are, the higher the probability that they are indeed correct. This relationship is known as the knowledge gradient.

knowledge-line (K-line) Theory that representations of items which are commonly encountered together are neurologically stored close together.

knowledge of results *Feedback* to a subject on the quality of his/her performance.

knowledge telling Recall of a large amount of knowledge without any apparent interpretation to shape it and make it comprehensible.

Knox Cubes Test A measure of *visuo-spatial* memory – the subject is required to tap cubes in a pattern provided by the experimenter.

Korsakoff's amnestic syndrome *Korsakoff's syndrome.*

Korsakoff's psychosis *Korsakoff's syndrome.*

Korsakoff's syndrome Profound *anterograde amnesia,* usually coupled with *confabulation.* Results from long-term vitamin deficiency, and is most often encountered in alcoholic patients.

Kosslyn's island task Experiment devised by Kosslyn et al. in which subjects are required to memorize a simple map of an island, and then mentally travel across sections of its *mental image.* Subjects' reported 'travel times' are typically proportional to the distances involved.

Kuhnian revolution Named after Thomas Kuhn, whose book, 'The Structure of Scientific Revolutions', postulates the process whereby sciences progresses, by moving from one *paradigm* to another by means of the *paradigm shift*.

L

labial (phonetics) Pertaining to a *phone* whose production involves the movement of one or both lips.

labiodental (phonetics) Pertaining to a *phone* whose production involves moving the bottom lip against the top teeth (e.g. the first sound in 'fish').

laboratory study See *ecological validity.*

LAD *language acquisition device.*

lag (1) The gap between the presentation of an item and its repetition. The lag can be measured in time, or in the number of other items the subject has been presented with between the two presentations. (2) The time for which an after-image can be seen.

Lana Chimpanzee taught to use a 'language' in which she chooses from a set of symbols representing different nouns and basic actions. The same technique has subsequently been applied to other chimpanzees, including **Sherman** and **Austin**. For general comments on language use, see *Washoe.*

language acquisition device (LAD) See *Chomsky's theory of language.*

language independence In computer programming, conceiving a programme without reference to a particular programming language. The phrase is sometimes extended to treating problems in abstract/symbolic terms, without regard to the specific materials used.

'last in, first out' *Ribot's hypothesis.*

LAT *lexical access time.*

late bottleneck theories See *bottleneck theories.*

late selection theory of attention *late bottleneck theory.*

latency *reaction time.*

lateral inhibition Phenomenon exhibited by some neurons, which in addition to sending a signal, also attempt to *inhibit* the signals sent by neighbouring neurons. The strength of the inhibition is greater the more excited the neuron is. The effect of this is that if a neuron is receiving a strong stimulus whilst its neighbours are receiving weak ones, the neuron will not only send a stronger signal per se, but also it will inhibit the neighbouring neurons more than they in turn can suppress it. This has the effect of exaggerating the signal even more. The result of lateral inhibition is that points of contrast where a weak and a strong stimulus meet are exaggerated. In *feed forward lateral inhibition*, the inhibition occurs not in the neurons concerned, but in the pathways over which signals are sent to the next set of neurons. In *recurrent lateral inhibition*, the inhibition occurs within the neurons, before any signals are sent out. The phenomenon is mimicked in some computerized models of mental functioning.

lateralization (-isation) The extent to which the left and right *hemispheres* share control of certain skills. For about 90% of right-handed people, the left hemisphere controls most verbal skills, and the right, most *visuo-spatial* skills. The reverse applies for about 60% of left-handers (i.e. left hemisphere = visuo-spatial, right = language). The remainder of subjects either display the 'wrong' asymmetry for their handedness, or displayed *functional symmetry* – i.e. the functions are spread across both hemispheres.

law of common fate *common fate.*

law of effect Rule devised by Thorndike which states that the likelihood of an action being repeated will increase if it has a positive outcome, and decrease if it is negative. See *law of practice.*

law of forgetting See *rate of forgetting.*

law of frequency The principle that the more an item is rehearsed, the greater the probability it will be remembered.

law of practice Rule devised by Thorndike which states that the more one rehearses a skill, the better it gets and the more likely it is to be repeated. See *law of effect.*

law of pragnanz *Gestalt* argument that the mind has a predisposition to perceive items as coherent wholes, and may mentally 'fill in' or 'smooth out' anomalies if this creates a whole figure (e.g. an incomplete figure may be perceived as whole even though it is not).

law of prior entry The phenomenon whereby, when presented with two stimuli occurring simultaneously, the subject will tend to cite the stimulus s/he was attending to at the time as occurring first.

law of recency (1) *recency effect.* (2) Generally, the phenomenon whereby recently-learnt information is more likely to be remembered than is older information.

law of repetition *law of frequency.*

layer (parallel distributed processing) Essentially, a particular process within a *parallel distributed processing* model,

with the *bottom layer* being the most basic (the one receiving the input) and the *top layer* usually being the most advanced (and presenting the output).

LCS *limited capacity stage.*

LDT *lexical decision task.*

learning curve The rate at which information about a topic is learnt. Typically (although not universally), this is a case of diminishing returns – a lot is learnt early in the study period, but progressively less new information is acquired the longer the person studies.

learning set *Einstellung.*

least mean squares (LMS) rule A method of *backward propagation.*

left-headed word See *right-headed word.*

legal error *preservation error.*

legal word See *illegal word.*

letter-by-letter reading *Acquired dyslexia* characterized by a failure to read words other than by reading them one letter at a time, and building the words up in this manner.

letter cancellation task Task in which the subject is given a display of letters and must strike out all examples of a particular letter or group of letters. The letters can be arranged in words and the words can form meaningful prose, which makes the test more difficult (see *proof reading errors*).

letter code Mental representation of letters.

letter identification span The field of view (the *total perceptual span*) from which information about letters is 'taken in'.

letter level See *level (mental model).*

letter matching task (1) Task in which the subject must judge if (usually two) letters are the same. (2) May refer specifically to the *Posner letter matching task.*

letter migration *letter migration error.*

letter migration error See *migration error.*

letter recognition unit Unit in a *mental model* responsible for collecting information, principally from *lower level units,* such as *feature detectors.* If the information collected is sufficiently akin to the letter it represents, then the unit fires, indicating recognition of that particular letter.

letter series completion test *Completion test* in which the subject must provide the next item(s) in a sequence of letters (e.g. A B C D...).

letter-sound conversion The process of converting printed letters into their spoken counterparts.

letter strings Groups of letters which may or may not form real words.

level (mental model) A particular hierarchical stage in a process. E.g. in models of reading, the *letter level* refers to the stage at which letters are identified, whilst the *word level* refers to the stage at which words are identified (largely from information supplied by the letter level).

level (of proposition) Roughly, the degree of importance a *proposition* (a statement or argument) has in the argument or story in question. E.g. in a story about a boy eating a cake stolen from the baker's shop, propositions concerning the theft and the eating would be high level propositions. Information about what the boy was wearing, or on which street the shop was, are not as central to the plot, and so are classed as lower-order propositions. Objectively and unambiguously deciding on the level of a proposition is fraught with difficulty, however, and usually there is considerable disagreement between subjects (or even experienced researchers) asked to codify a piece of text in this manner.

level of activation Concept widely used in *mental models.* It is well documented that, if suitably *primed,* some processes respond faster to a stimulus (see e.g. *semantic facilitation*). Level of activation denotes the state of 'excitement' a unit in a mental model is in. The more primed it is, the higher its level of activation is said to be, and the less excitation it requires to prod it into action. The level of activation the unit experiences when it is unstimulated is called the **resting level of activation.** Some models assume that e.g. frequently used items have a higher resting level, making them easier to move past the *threshold.* Confusingly, the level of excitation at which activation occurs (i.e. the threshold) is sometimes called the **activation level.** However, note that the same term is also used as a synonym of *level of activation.*

levelling In recalling a story, lengthy piece of prose, etc., the omission of extraneous detail.

levels of processing A model of memory (first suggested by Craik and Lockhart, although subsequently elaborated in several forms – e.g. the **cognitive space model** and the *dual coding theory*) which argues that items can be encoded in several ways (e.g. in terms of visual appearance, meaning, sound, etc.), and that the more levels of processing an item receives, the better it is remembered. Information which is processed towards a deeper level is said to undergo **type II processing,** whilst information which is simply being retained in memory without further analysis is said to undergo **type I processing.** At a descriptive level at least the model is usually an accurate representation of events (e.g. lists of words which have been examined to see if they sound like a given example are remembered less well than those which have been examined for their semantic properties, because the latter involves a greater degree of processing). However, the theoretical justification has been disputed, not least because there is no truly objective measure of processing depth. In part, the theory arose out of dissatisfaction with *storage models of memory*, which some commentators felt unduly emphasized *mnemonic* storage mechanisms at the expense of discussion of how memories are formed.

lexical access The process of accessing information stored in a *lexicon* (particularly a *mental lexicon*). The time taken to do this is called the **lexical access time**.

lexical access time (LAT) See *lexical access*.

lexical ambiguity See *homograph*.

lexical analogy pronunciation model Model of pronunciation of read words, which assumes that knowledge of pronunciation of sequences of letters within a word is combined with knowledge of whole words in the same process. See *dual route pronunciation model*.

lexical decision task (LDT) A very heavily used psychological experimental method. Subjects are shown *letter strings* and asked to judge as quickly as possible whether the strings form real words. Note that the subjects do not have to judge what a discovered real word 'says'.

lexical decision time Time taken to perform a *lexical decision task*.

lexical dysgraphia *surface dysgraphia.*

lexical frequency *word frequency.*

lexical item An item ('word') in a *mental lexicon.*

lexical membership Membership of a *mental lexicon.*

lexical memory Memory for words (usually the term is restricted to memory for the visual and phonological features of the word, rather than its meaning).

lexical status *lexical membership.*

lexical uncertainty The brief pause in speech before pronunciation of rare or new words.

lexicon (1) The total words which comprise a particular language. (2) *mental lexicon.*

light-bulb problem Problem akin to the *Wason card task* in which the subject are told that light bulbs will break if heated above a certain temperature. They are then given four conditions – an intact light-bulb, a broken light-bulb, and two temperatures (above and below the critical 'breaking temperature') and asked which conditions must be examined to test the rule.

likelihood ratio The ratio of the likelihood that an item belongs to group A as opposed to group B.

limited capacity stage (LCS) Stage in any process which has a limited *capacity.*

linear ordering phenomenon The phenomenon whereby, when a subject has learnt a list, recall is slower (i) when items have to be recalled other than in the order in which they were learnt; or (ii) where the item following on from a given item has to be provided, recall is slower the further into the list the item in question appears. There is some amelioration of the effects in condition (i) if the items at the start of the list match the original list ordering (***front anchor-***

ing) or if the end of the list matches (*end anchoring*).

linear process The phenomenon whereby a rise in the value of one item is always met with a rise or always with a fall in the value of another unit, and when the relationship is expressed as a graph, a straight line is produced. In a *nonlinear process*, either the line on the graph is curved, or changes in one item are not always met with changes in the other (e.g. past a certain value of x, y might have reached maximum output, and therefore produce the same response no matter by how much more x increases).

linguistic awareness The conscious awareness of one's linguistic skills, and of how language is structured. See *phonemic awareness*.

linguistic competence The possession of a full set of rules of language, which would enable the subject, given the vocabulary, to create any possible statement in the language in question. See *performance (linguistics)*.

linguistic performance *performance (linguistics)*.

linguistic register The set of words that a person habitually uses, which may relate to their environment/community.

linguistic relativity hypothesis The hypothesis that one's perception of the world is constrained by the language one uses. The often-cited example is that Westerners have lots of words for types of cars, and hence, it is argued, they can perceive more types of cars than e.g. some people from non-industrialized societies who have only a limited number of words for modes of transport. The strong form of the argument is virtually untenable, because it is intuitively more likely that we create words to describe our experiences (e.g. we have lots of words for cars because we have seen so many different types). The weaker, and more tenable form of the argument is that language shapes thought, even if it does not create it. See *Dani tribe*.

linguistic universals The basic properties shared by all languages.

Linton diary study *Diary study* of *autobiographical memory* by Linton, who kept a diary of her daily life, and at varying intervals tested her recall of events, comparing them with the diary record.

LISP Programming language used in some *artificial intelligence* programmes.

literal dyslexia *attentional dyslexia*.

Lloyd Morgan's canon Argument that behaviour should be explained in terms of the *lowest level* processes which can accommodate it.

LMS rule *least mean squares (LMS) rule*.

LNR Pronounced 'Elinor'. Computerized memory model (particularly of *semantic memory*).

lobe A segment of the cortex. The four major lobes are the *frontal lobe, parietal lobe, occipital lobe*, and *temporal lobe*.

local (problem solving) The features of the problem at one particular stage in the solving process. This contrasts with the *global state*, which is the overall requirement of the problem (which does not consider the specific details of the stages required to do this).

local coherence The degree to which succeeding sentences or statements make sense when presented together.

local feature See *feature*.

local minima (parallel distributed processing) See *gradient descent (parallel distributed processing)*.

local network model *network model*.

local representation See *distributed representation*.

locative case See *case grammar*.

logical inference *Inference* that a word or argument is used in its conventional sense (e.g. if a 'man' is mentioned, it is assumed that he will not give birth).

logogen In some models of mental functioning, a unit representing verbal items. The logogen is usually regarded as an 'evidence collector' – once a certain number of features have been identified then a *threshold* is passed, and the item is identified. See *imagen*.

logogen model A *mental model* of word recognition and production, which is composed of basic units called *logogens*.

logogram The representation of a word by a symbol.

logographic writing Writing system in which each spoken word is represented by a unique written symbol.

logography *logographic writing*.

long-term memory (LTM) (1) The total knowledge which a subject has encoded for permanent storage in his/her mind. (2) The mechanisms controlling the same. Not all this knowledge can be retrieved, however (whether it has been erased, or is still there but is no longer accessible to retrieval strategies has been lengthily debated – see *threshold hypothesis*). LTM can be itemized according to the nature of the information being encoded (e.g. *autobiographical memory, episodic memory, semantic memory,* etc.). Note that some commentators distinguish between the long-term memory store itself and the mechanisms used to encode and retrieve information – see *long-term store*. LTM's functions and physiological substrates are often viewed in contrast with those of *short-term memory*. See *long-term store*.

long-term span See *span*.

long-term store (LTS) See *short-term store*.

loop avoidance strategy Problem-solving strategy in which the subject attempts to avoid returning to an earlier stage in the problem-solving process.

low association See *association*.

low density neighbourhood See *neighbours*.

low frequency words See *frequency (words)*.

low level process Relatively 'primitive' process responsible for a basic 'building block' of a task. This contrasts with a **high level process**, which is responsible for, or receives the integration of, information from lower level processes. E.g. in reading, a low level process might be letter recognition, whilst a high level process might be extracting meaning from a sentence or phrase. The terms are frequently used very loosely, often as a conceptual shorthand.

low level proposition *microproposition*.

low level schema See *schema theory*.

low level unit Unit involved in a *low level process*.

lower case See *case*.

lower level process *low level process*.

L.P. Neurological patient in an often-cited case study, who had a severe difficulty in defining words.

LTM *long-term memory*.

LTS *long-term store*.

M

machine intelligence See *artificial intelligence*.

machine metaphor Any *metaphor of mental functioning* in which brain processes are related to the workings of a machine (e.g. the *computational metaphor of the mind*).

machine vision Use of *artificial intelligence* to perform visual perception tasks.

macroproposition A principal detail of a piece of text or argument which forms part of its gist or essential plot. See *macrostructure* and *microproposition*.

macrorule A rule governing the extraction of a *macroproposition*.

macrospotlight See *microspotlight*.

macrostructure The essential structure of a piece of text or argument – i.e. its 'gist' or essence. See *macroproposition*.

Magical Number Seven A journal article, 'The magical number seven, plus or minus two: Some limits on our capacity for processing information', by G. Miller. The paper argues that in the short term, most people can accurately remember or process between five and nine *chunks* of information, with a mean of seven.

magnetic resonance imaging (MRI) A method of scanning an organ (e.g. the brain), producing three-dimensional images. It involves placing the body in a strong magnetic field, then switching the field off. This causes the cells to release radio waves which can be read and interpreted by the MRI scanner.

maintenance rehearsal See *rehearsal*.

MANIAC Chess playing computer programme.

manikin test Any test in which the subject must fit together the pieces of a model of a human body.

mapping (1) Matching items belonging to two or more sets. E.g. deciding if an item in front of one (i.e. a member of a *display set*) is identical to an item in memory (i.e. a member of a *memory set*). (2) How areas of the body are represented by areas of the brain. See *consistent mapping*.

MARGIE Computer programme by Schank and Abelson which uses a preprogrammed *schema* to interpret a piece of text on an appropriately related topic. The text is broken down into *conceptual dependencies*.

Marker-Search model A *network model* in which items are linked with 'defining markers' which indicate the properties held by the item (e.g. 'tulip' might have a defining marker of 'flower' which has the properties of leaves, petals, etc.).

Marr's computational theory Theory of visual perception by the late Marr, who argued that a visual image passes through a series of processing stages, or *representations*. These include the *primal sketch*, which essentially identifies contours, patterns of light and shade, etc. The *2.5-D sketch* is a representation of the distance and orientation of parts of objects, and the *3-D model representation* is the final representation.

mask See *masking*.

masking The technique of destroying or impairing one image by the superimposition of another (a *mask*). This can be sub-classified according to when the masking took place. In *backward masking*, the mask is presented just after the target stimulus. In *forward masking*, the mask appears just before the target stimulus. Masking can also be classified according to the senses involved. E.g. *auditory masking* refers to playing one sound to impair perception or processing of another. *Visual masking* is the presentation of a visual stimulus to impair the perception or processing of another. There are several forms which this can take. *Brightness masking* consists of presenting a bright light just before or after the target. This impairs the retina's ability to register the object. *Pattern masking* is the presentation of a mask consisting of a pattern. It is known to affect *cortical* processing of the image. In *pattern masking by noise*, the pattern consists of a random pattern (typically, black and white dots/squares, akin to the screen of an untuned TV set). In *pattern masking by structure*, the pattern contains elements which are similar in appearance to the target stimulus. In *metacontrast masking*, the target item is briefly displayed, and is then replaced by a mask (also briefly displayed) which surrounds the contours of the target, but does not overlap it. *Paracontrast masking* is identical, save that the mask is displayed before the target stimulus is presented. See *stimulus onset asynchrony*.

masking theory Any theory which attributes a decline in performance to the effect of one stimulus being *masked* by another.

mass action Theory devised by Lashley which states that memories are represented by a widespread pattern of activation in the *cortex*, and not just excitation in a very small section of it.

massed practice See *distribution of practice*.

Mastermind (1) Principally an American term for a game in which one player must deduce the combination and sequence of coloured pegs his/her opponent has placed in a line hidden from view. This is done by producing a line of coloured pegs intended to replicate the hidden line. The player is told how many colours and positions s/he has correctly replicated. By repeating this process with different lines, and paying attention to the feedback, the player should be able to deduce the line within the limited number of moves available. In experimental situations, the game has been used to test logical skills. (2) In Britain, the name of a long-running TV quiz show, with (by television standards) very difficult general knowledge questions.

matching bias In solving a *conditional reasoning* problem (e.g. the *Wason card task*) having an (erroneous) bias towards choosing items akin to those mentioned in the original problem, rather than truly testing the rule in question (e.g. in assessing the rule 'if x, then y', only considering x and y).

McGurk effect Phenomenon generated by displaying a film/video tape of a person articulating one *phoneme*, whilst the soundtrack plays another phoneme. Subjects tend to report hearing neither the 'visual phoneme' nor the 'auditory phoneme' but a 'blend' of the two.

McMAP An *artificial intelligence* model of sentence comprehension.

M.D. Neurological patient in an often-cited case study, with the remarkable deficiency of being unable to define fruit and vegetables, although other objects were accurately described.

meaning-based representation
Representation of an item in terms of its relevance, rather than its appearance. This contrasts with *perception-based representation*, which is the representation of an item in terms of its appearance rather than its relevance per se.

means-ends analysis A problem-solving method in which the discrepancy between the *initial state* and the *goal state* is examined, and the steps necessary to remove this difference are calculated. This often involves establishing a set of *sub-goals*.

mechanization of thought *Einstellung.*

mediation Rather nebulous term denoting a mental process which represents events in a symbolic system different from the original. E.g. *verbal mediation* is a representation of events in a linguistic code.

medical student effect The phenomenon whereby some medical students gain the (mis)apprehension that they are suffering from the disease they are studying. By extension, the misperception that because one is learning about something (usually unpleasant), that it applies to oneself.

memorist *mnemonist.*

memory capacity (1) *span.* (2) *mental capacity.*

memory load *memory set.*

memory organization (-isation) packet (MOP) A collection of several *scripts*, which together enable a person to act appropriately in a specific situation (e.g. going to the dentist, going shopping, etc.). MOPs may have scripts in common

(e.g. going to the dentist and going shopping share a script for paying for goods or services). Rather than waste *memory space* with storing an identical script in each MOP, it makes intuitive sense to keep a 'mental library' of scripts, which can be drawn upon for different situations. This may explain why people tend to confuse events whose MOPs have a lot of scripts in common (e.g. visits to a zoo and to a park). MOPs can be joined together to form *metaMOPs*, which are a conglomeration of several smaller MOPs (e.g. a day out metaMOP may call upon a driving MOP, a shopping MOP, a visiting an ancestral house MOP, a bad weather MOP, etc.). See *thematic organization packet.*

memory search The process of searching one's memory for a *target* item. See *backward memory search* and *forward memory search*.

memory set The total set of items which a subject is requested to remember.

memory space *memory capacity.*

memory span *span.*

memory trace The storage of a memory.

mental capacity The limit on how much information a mind can process at any one time, and/or how quickly it can process information. The term is a useful conceptual notion, but producing an objective, accurate measure of it is often impossible. It can be estimated, however, and it is known that it differs between individuals (more intelligent people can process more information at a faster rate), and within individuals across time (e.g. capacity often declines in old age).

mental effort The degree to which a subject must attend to the task in question.

mental imagery A mental representation of a physical object or event, which is subjectively felt to be a 'picture in the head'. Whether the mind can process information directly from the mental image, or whether it is simply a by-product of the mental apparatus which actually performs the processing is a matter of some debate (see *analogue representation* and *propositional representation*). See *grain size*.

mental lexicon The total set of words (and in some theories non-word sounds as well) which a subject possesses in his/her 'mental store', (and in some models their attendant definitions also). In some theories of linguistic processing, the mental lexicon is imagined to be like a library which is searched through for the correct word. See *auditory lexicon*. The lexicon can be used to comprehend input (*input lexicon*) or to produce output (*output lexicon*).

mental map A *mental image* of a geographical area or physical space. The map is not necessarily literal, and it may for example exaggerate features which interest the subject, and diminish those which do not.

mental model A representation of a thought process by symbolic means (often a flow diagram, or latterly, a computer programme). Examples of mental models abound in psychology, and in cognition in particular (e.g. the *working memory* model).

mental processes The hypothesized methods by which information is encoded, processed and retrieved. This is contrasted with ***mental structures***, which are the hypothesized contents and structures of mental stores.

mental representation The memory of an object or event, which is used to gauge whether a perception is a representation of the object or event in question (e.g. whether a perception of a red, roughly round object on top of a green vertical object corresponds with a mental representation of a carnation).

mental rotation Manipulating a mental image of an item to 'see' it mentally in another orientation. Common methods of assessing this include giving the subject a letter or letter-like shape in an unusual orientation, and asking them to rotate it mentally to an upright orientation to judge if it is a real letter. Another popular method is the *Shepard mental rotation task*.

mental size The subjectively-perceived size of a piece of *mental imagery*.

mental structures See *mental processes*.

mental walk (1) Making a mental tour of a mental image of a real life object or scene. (2) As (1), but with the express intent of finding an object mislaid in real life in the scene being represented in the mind. (3) The process of scanning a mental image in the *method of loci* technique.

message level In a communication, the level of interpretation at which the intent of the message is processed.

meta- The prefix usually denotes 'overall', or, when it prefixes a name of a skill, an understanding of the skill in question. Usually it is implied that it is an understanding of how one's own mental skills work, rather than a more global understanding. See e.g. *metacognition*.

metacognition Knowledge of how one's cognitive abilities function.

metacomprehension Knowledge of how one's abilities to comprehend (particularly a passage of prose) function.

metacontrast masking See *masking*.

metaknowledge *epistemic awareness.* See *feeling of knowing.*

metalearning (1) study skills. (2) knowledge of how one learns and how learning can be optimized.

metalinguistic awareness Awareness of how the rules of a language operate.

metamemory A person's knowledge of their own mnemonic abilities – their strengths and weaknesses, their capacity, methods of making to-be-remembered items more memorable, etc. See the more specialized terms *epistemic awareness, feeling of knowing* and *systemic awareness.*

metamemory inference *Inference* about the validity of a *proposition* using *metamemory* as a basis for this reasoning.

metaMOP See *memory organization packet.*

metaphor of mental functioning
Using the image of a mechanism whose workings are relatively well understood as a metaphor of mental functioning, which is less well comprehended. The aim is to aid understanding by looking for analogies between the functions of that which is known and the more mysterious workings of the mind. A variety of mechanisms have been used as analogies. The currently popular model is the *computational metaphor of the mind*, in which the workings of a computer are likened to those of the mind. Previously, a variety of other technological devices have been used (e.g. clockwork, steam engines, etc.).

metareading What a person knows of their own reading abilities and of the reading process itself. See *phonemic awareness.*

method of loci technique A *mnemonic* aid in which a list of to-be-remembered items are mentally placed at different locations in a mental image of a familiar place. E.g. suppose one had to remember the digit list '1453'. One might imagine one's living room – the 1 is sitting in an armchair, the 4 is closing the curtains, etc. See *keyword technique, peg-word system* and *Simonides of Ceos.*

method of vanishing cues Method of learning a piece of information in which the number of *cues* necessary to elicit recall are progressively lowered until it can be recalled without any cues.

microproposition A minor detail of a text, which does not constitute part of its essential plot or gist. Compare with *macroproposition.*

microspotlight An *attention spotlight* focused upon a very narrow range of items. This contrasts with a *macrospotlight*, which is concerned with a comparatively wider range.

microworld An aspect of the 'real world' which is represented in a *mental model.*

migration error Error in which parts of an item are misperceived as belonging to another item (i.e. as if features of the items have 'migrated'). The phenomenon is seen in e.g. reporting items seen in a *tachistoscope*. A *letter migration error* occurs when subjects report a blend of two words in a display (e.g. display contains 'camel' and 'rabbit'; subject reports 'cat').

mind–body problem The debate as to whether the mind is distinct from the body (and in particular, the brain) and if so, how the two relate to one another. The issue, first proposed by the early philosophers, is deceptively simple, but no completely satisfactory solution has been discovered (consult a general text on philosophy for a lengthy exposition of this subject).

mirror drawing task Task in which a subject must draw a design whilst only able to see the results of his/her efforts through a mirror.

miscue An error (particulary of reading). The term is particularly applied to children's reading errors.

missionaries and cannibals problem See *river crossing problem*.

mixed brainedness (hemispheres) *functional symmetry*.

mixed dominance (hemispheres) *functional symmetry*.

mixed transcortical aphasia *Aphasia* in which virtually all linguistic abilities have been lost, barring the ability to repeat single words.

mMOP *metaMOP*.

mnemonic (1) Pertaining to memory. (2) *mnemonic aid*.

mnemonic aid A method of aiding memory (e.g. the initial letters of the phrase 'Richard of York gave battle in vain' give the colours of the rainbow).

mnemonist A person with an exceptionally good memory.

modal memory model Model of memory first proposed by Atkinson and Shiffrin. At the heart of the model is a *short-term store*. This receives input from a series of sensory registers, and acts as a 'relay station' to encode information for storage in a *long-term store*, and to retrieve it. The short-term store is also responsible for rehearsing information, and producing information for output.

modal recall (1) The most common response to a particular question or task. (2) Recalling an item as an amalgam of features, not necessarily in their correct relative positions.

modality effect (1) The relative advantage of processing/memorizing information presented in one modality over another. (2) The term is sometimes used specifically to denote that the last few items in a spoken list are remembered better than the same items in a written list.

mode error Error resulting from a misperception of the demands of the situation.

modular architecture The structure of a *modular system*.

modular psychology The belief that the mind consists of a collection of modules, specializing in specific tasks, which are functionally independent of each other. Compare with *unitary psychology*.

modular system A system which is composed of a number of sub-systems, each doing a task separate from the workings of the others. This is contrasted with a *non-modular system*, in which the sub-systems are not fully independent, and are reliant on each other and/or a *central processor*. The terminology is derived from computing.

modularity The degree to which a system resembles a *modular system*.

modus ponens The inference that given 'if A then B', then if A is true, B is true. See *modus tollens*.

modus tollens The inference that given 'if A then B', then if B is false, A is false. See *modus ponens*.

monocular depth cue Information about the depth of an object (i.e. how far away it is) which can be perceived with just one eye. By contrast, *binocular depth cues* are pieces of information about depth which are only available when looking with two eyes.

monotonic function A process in which each item is either always bigger or smaller than the one before.

monster problem Problem in which there are three globes (one small, one medium and one large) and three monsters (small, medium and large). The subject must exchange globes between monsters so that the monster has the appropriate globe (i.e. small monster has small globe, medium monster has medium globe, large monster has large globe). One globe can be moved at a time, with two provisos: (i) no monster may receive a globe smaller than the one it is already holding, and (ii) if a monster is holding two globes, only the larger one may be moved.

mood congruency Phenomenon whereby one tends to recall some events (particularly *autobiographical memories*) in a mood befitting one's current emotional state. E.g. a party might be recalled as enjoyable when in a happy state, but as an occasion of wretched sexual failure when one is depressed. See *mood-state dependency*.

mood-state dependency The phenomenon whereby information is better recalled when the subject is in the same emotional state s/he was in when the information was first learnt. See *mood congruency*.

MOP *Memory Organization Packet.*

morpheme The smallest unit of a word whose addition or removal alters the word's meaning (e.g. 'illegible' contains two morphemes – 'il' and 'legible'). See *root morpheme* and *bound morpheme*. See *allomorph* and *compound word*.

morpheme exchange error Error in which the *root morphemes* of two words in a statement are exchanged (e.g. 'the kickball was footed'). Not to be confused with a *Spoonerism*.

morphological Pertaining to *morphemes*.

morphology Strictly speaking, the science of form. Also, an awareness of word meanings and word structure.

motor aphasia *Broca's aphasia.*

motor area An area of the *frontal lobe* involved in movement control.

motor code See *motor representation*.

motor cortex *motor area.*

motor representation The storage of information about movement. The *encoding* of this information uses **motor code**.

motor theory of speech perception Theory that speech perception involves many of the processes involved in speech production.

MOVE problems Problem-solving tasks characterized by the need to move items from one location to another (e.g. the *Tower of Hanoi problem* and the *water jar problem*).

movement schema A sequence of movements appropriate to a particular situation.

moving window technique (1) Experimental technique in which the subject is given only a partial view of a display through a 'window' moving over it. To gain an accurate perception of the whole display, the subject must remember and accumulate information seen in successive fragments. (2) In a permutation of (1), a method of *paced reading*. The subject must read an otherwise hidden text as it is revealed by a window passing over it. (3) A method of assessing *perceptual span*. Subjects are shown a display, and items around the *fixation position* are altered. The perceptual span is defined as the area within which such changes are noticed.

MRI *magnetic resonance imaging.*

MTRANS See *primitive action*.

multi-modal model (learning) M o d e l of memory/learning which emphasizes that these skills will not improve unless wider aspects of lifestyle as well as different facets of memory are considered and improved.

multi-store memory model Model of memory in which memory is represented as a set of several functionally distinct *mnemonic* processes. Usually the term refers to the *three store memory model.*

multichannel processing P r o c e s s i n g more than two or more pieces of information simultaneously (what constitutes a 'piece of information' has caused much debate).

multiple resource theory Theory that more than one type of processing and/or source of *mental capacity* is available.

multiprocessor procedure *multichannel processing.*

mutilated chess board problem A measure of problem-solving ability. A subject is told (truthfully) that, given thirty-two dominoes, each of which covers two squares of a chess board, it is possible to cover all sixty-four squares of the board. If the two black corner squares of the board are removed, is it possible to cover what is left of the board with thirty-one dominoes? There are variants of this problem.

mutually exclusive event Event whose outcome excludes the occurrence of another event (e.g. if a coin lands 'heads', then this excludes 'tails' and vice versa – hence 'heads' and 'tails' are mutually exclusive events).

mutually independent event *m u t u a l l y exclusive event.*

MYCIN *Artificial intelligence* programme which diagnoses the strain of bacteria causing an infection, and from this, the best course of treatment.

N

N.A. Neurological patient in an often-cited case study, with a severe failure to retain any information learnt since his accident in *long-term memory*.

name identity (NI) task See *Posner letter matching task*.

naming latency The *reaction time* taken to name a word or item.

narremic substitution Misreading a word but maintaining the narrative thread of the text.

NART *National Adult Reading Test*.

nasal (phonetics) Pertaining to a *phone* whose production involves the exhalation of air through the nose.

National Adult Reading Test (NART) A list of words, most with *irregular spellings*, which the subject is required to read out loud (i.e. to pronounce). The more words correctly pronounced, the higher the test score.

natural category A category which seems to accord with innate perceptions (e.g. it seems intuitively obvious to place birds in one category and land animals in another). A phenomenon associated with this is that less typical members of a category are harder to accept as members (e.g. for Westerners it takes longer to decide that a yam is a vegetable than it does for a potato). See *artificial category* and *basic level category*.

natural knowledge Knowledge about everyday life. This contrasts with **technical knowledge**, which is knowledge derived from learning a specific skill or body of information.

natural language Language as it is usually spoken by native speakers.

natural language mediator *Mnemonic* strategy in which a list of to-be-remembered items are made to fit a simple story or sentence (e.g. in learning about music, the phrase 'every good boy deserves food' indicates the notes E,G,B,D,F on the treble clef).

naturalistic psychology Psychological investigations with a high level of *ecological validity*.

necklace problem *cheap necklace problem*.

negative feedback See *feedback*.

negative memory A 'memory' that something has not occurred (more accurately, an ability to recognize that a particular memory does not exist).

negative recognition *negative memory*.

negative set See *positive set*.

negative transfer Impaired performance resulting from prior experience of another task. E.g. transferring from playing the descant to the treble recorder can be difficult because the same fingering patterns produce different notes in the two instruments. See *proactive interference* and *retroactive interference*.

negatively accelerated change A change whose rate diminishes over time (i.e. there are big increases/decreases at the beginning, but small increases/decreases later). The term is sometimes used to describe the *rate of forgetting*.

neighbourhood See *neighbours*.

neighbours (1) Items which resemble another item (e.g. by having similar features). The collection of neighbours is called a *neighbourhood*, and the number of items in it is measured by its density. A *high density neighbourhood* contains a lot of similar items, whilst a *low density neighbourhood* possesses relatively few. (2) Items close to each other in a display.

'Neisser's Law' Dictum of Ulric Neisser,[*] a celebrated cognitive psychologist – 'If X is an important or interesting feature of human behavior, then X has rarely been studied by psychologists'.

NETtalk *Parallel distributed processing* programme which converts text into speech, and will learn pronunciations of words it has not previously encountered.

network model Term given to a wide range of models of mental functioning which attempt to explain how associations between different items can be made and hence form a network of connections. See *semantic network*.

neural computing Any *neurocomputational* process.

neural net *neural network*.

neural network The basic structure of a *parallel distributed processing* model.

neurocomputational Pertaining to any *artificial intelligence* model in which the operations of the electrical circuitry and/or programmes mimic the workings of the nervous system. The term is more or less synonymous with *parallel distributed processing*.

new information (linguistics) See *given-new contract*.

NI task *name identity task*.

Nim See *Washoe*.

nine dot problem Problem solving task demonstrating *functional fixedness*. Subjects are shown a 3 x 3 matrix of dots (which form a square shape), and are asked to draw four lines covering all the dots, with the proviso that the pencil cannot leave the paper in drawing the lines. Subjects often fail the test because they (erroneously) suppose that the pencil cannot leave the confines of the square. The solution involves drawing lines outside the bounds of the square.

NOAH Computerized problem-solving programme.

node In many models of e.g. linguistic or mental functioning, the process is represented as a series of pathways (representing different options for processing) which converge and diverge away from meeting points, where information from the different processes is gathered together, or a decision is made about which processing step should be performed next. These junction points are called 'nodes'.

noetic Term coined by Tulving to denote the level of conscious awareness a subject has of a particular mental process. This can range from *anoetic* (requiring no conscious awareness) to *autonoetic* (fully dependent on conscious awareness).

noise (1) Unwanted sound or signals. (2) Random neural activity which can be confused with a genuine signal (see *signal detection analysis*).

---

[*] (Neisser, U. (1978) 'Memory: What are the important questions?' In M.M. Gruneberg et al. (eds) *Practical Aspects of Memory*. London: Academic Press, p.2)

non-adversarial problem See *adversarial problem*.

non-fluent aphasia *Broca's aphasia*, or more generally, any *expressive aphasia*.

non-modular system See *modular system*.

non-response (NR) Simply, not responding to a stimulus. The term is sometimes used of an (allegedly) characteristic phase of children's reading skills, in which the majority of errors take the form of non-responses, rather than misreadings of words, etc.

non-semantic reading *demented dyslexia*.

nonfocal colour See *focal colour*.

nonlinear process See *linear process*.

nonsense syllable Any syllable which does not form a real word.

nonsense words (1) Words which are not recognizably part of the language when spoken or written (of which *pseudowords* are a special case). (2) Words which are not recognizable when written, but when spoken aloud, sound like a real word (e.g. 'phrock'). Such words can only be read by 'sounding them out'. See *illegal word*.

nonstrategic processing *incidental learning*.

nontarget *distractor item*.

nonword *nonsense word*.

norm-based recognition Recognizing an item by comparing it with a *prototype*.

noun phrase (NP) A portion of a sentence which describes the *subject* or *object*. See *verb phrase (VP)*.

NP *noun phrase*.

NR *non-response*.

number series completion test *Completion test* in which the subject must provide the next item(s) in a sequence of numbers (e.g. 1 3 9 ...).

number series problem Measure of problem-solving ability. Subjects are presented with a three digit sequence (e.g. 3,6,9), and are asked to give another three digit sequence which obeys the same rules. Subjects generate examples, and are told if they are correct.

O

object (linguistics) See *subject (linguistics)*.

object concept Not surprisingly, a concept of an object. This contrasts with *relational concepts*, which are concepts of relations between items.

object permanence The knowledge that an object continues to exist when the senses can no longer detect it. According to some theories, this knowledge needs to be learnt during infancy (i.e. it is not innate). There is a long and very tedious philosophical debate on whether we can ever be logically certain that objects exist when they cannot be perceived.

object recognition The ability to recognize objects. Some commentators restrict the term to recognition of three-dimensional objects, others to all visual stimuli (therefore also including two-dimensional objects, such as letters, words, patterns, etc.).

object superiority effect Phenomenon whereby an item can usually be identified faster when it is an appropriate part of a larger object than when it is presented in isolation. The best known example of this is the *word superiority effect*.

objective case See *case grammar*.

objective test (1) Test whose questions have definite right and wrong answers. (2) Test which, in its marking, is not reliant on subjective interpretation. Some commentators add the additional caveat that the subjects must not be able to discern the purpose of the test (hence preventing biased responses, in an at-tempt to create a favourable impression). See *open-ended test*.

objective threshold See *threshold*.

objectivity (of test) The degree to which a test is immune to the subjective biases of the person administering or taking it.

oblique effect Phenomenon whereby parallel fine lines are seen better when they are vertical or horizontal than when they are angled.

oBOSS See *BOSS*.

observer memories The phenomenon whereby one's distant *autobiographical memories* are usually recalled with the subjective impression of being a by-stander.

Occam's razor *parsimony principle*. Named after William of Occam (1285–1349), medieval philosopher.

occipital lobes The region of the *cerebral cortex* roughly located at 'the back of the head'. Their principal function is in visual perception.

on-line awareness Monitoring current mental performance.

on-line processing Manipulating the processing of an item while the process is taking place (as opposed to e.g. processing an item, assessing the results, and altering the processing when the next item is dealt with).

onset (syllable) See *syllable*.

opaque A term used loosely to denote something which is hard to process. This is in contrast with the term *transparent*, denoting something which is easy to process. See *opaque system*.

opaque system A mental process which cannot be assessed by *introspection*. This contrasts with a **transparent system**, whose operation can at least in part be checked by introspection, and from this, modified.

open-ended question See *close-ended question*.

open-ended test Test whose answers cannot be objectively classified as definitely right, or definitely wrong. E.g. a question such as 'what is the capital of the United Kingdom?' has only one correct answer. However, a question such as 'how can one solve the ills of the British economy?' is open-ended, because there is a practically infinite range of answers. Contrast with *objective test*.

open loop processes *Automatic processes.* See also *closed loop processes*.

open set (knowledge) A group of facts which can be added to (e.g. known stars in the universe). Compare with *closed set (knowledge)*.

open system Any system which is affected by external forces.

openness The capacity for a language to express new concepts, assimilate new vocabulary, etc.

operator In a *mental model*, the process which transforms data from one format into another.

operator selection Choosing the appropriate action/tools to accomplish a *subgoal*.

opposites test Any measure in which the subject must either (i) supply the opposite of a word presented by the experimenter, or (ii) identify pairs of opposites from a list of alternatives.

optic flow pattern See *Gibson's theory of direct perception*.

orbital cortex Area of *frontal lobe* responsible, inter alia, for controlling social behaviour, observing proprieties, etc.

orcs and hobbits problem See *river crossing problem*.

ordered recall *serial recall.*

O.R.F. Neuropsychological patient in an often-cited case study, who had relative difficulty in processing *nonsense words*.

orienting task Task which prepares/orients a subject towards a further task.

orthographic Pertaining to *orthography*.

orthographic lexicon A *mental lexicon* of *orthography*. E.g. knowledge of spelling patterns.

orthographic regularity The degree to which a word contains sequences of letters in common usage, independent of considerations of how the word and/or letter groups are pronounced. See *regular spelling*.

orthographic priming *Priming* in which the *prime* is a word which contains letters in common with the *target item*.

orthography A visual language (i.e. writing and printing).

output lexicon Any *mental lexicon* responsible for producing an output (particularly speech and writing).

output modality Format in which the subject's response is presented (e.g. spoken, written, etc.).

output processes See *information processing*.

outside-inside processing *bottom-up processing.*

overlapping tasks paradigm Experimental method in which different items are presented to the subject for processing either overlapping in temporal sequence or in very rapid succession.

overlearned skill A skill which has been practised for a considerable period after it has already been learnt to a high standard of performance.

overload *cognitive overload.*

overspill coding *Encoding* which takes place although the subject may not intend to do it (e.g. in a task in which one is asked to remember a list of words, one is aware of what the words mean, even though one has been asked simply to remember the words).

own-race bias Phenomenon whereby under some conditions, people are more accurate at processing information about members of their own race/cultural group (e.g. many instances of face recognition).

P

paced reading Any method in which the subject is required to read at a pace set by the experimenter (e.g. definition (2) of *moving window technique*).

palindrome A word or phrase which is the same when read in either direction (e.g. 'radar').

PAM *pre-categorical acoustic memory.*

Pandemonium model Model of pattern recognition (principally concentrating on letter recognition). It was created by Selfridge and developed by Lindsay and Norman. The model was composed of various *recognition units* which the authors called *demons*. It was the combination of *excitation* of these units which identified the pattern being seen. E.g. suppose the model was presented with the letter 'S'. This is composed of curves, and so the demons which respond to curves would be excited. However, the demons which respond to straight lines would remain unexcited. There are only three upper case letters which have curves and no straight lines – C, O and S. Further demons are then used to identify the types of angles and the patterns which the identified lines form. This is sufficient to identify the letter as 'S'. The term 'pandemonium' describes the mass of excitation which occurs when a pattern is first processed – since many letters share at least some features in common, lots of the demons will be initially excited, before a clearer picture emerges. The model is a pleasing one (not least for the pictures of demons in the authors' illustrations), and was hugely influential. It is now recognized as being too simplistic, but it formed the basis of many subsequent models.

paracontrast masking See *masking.*

paradigm (1) A basic theory around which a substantial body of research and other theories are based. (2) In the work of Thomas Kuhn the term denotes the accepted theories which determine how researchers view a particular field. Since paradigms change over time (see *paradigm failure* and *paradigm shift*), this argues that what is regarded as 'good' and 'bad' research and further, what constitutes a valid proof may be dictated by the *zeitgeist* rather than the objective search for ultimate truths (e.g. Aristotle and Newton were pre-eminent in their own paradigms, but have been proven wrong on many things according to more modern theories).

paradigm failure Term coined by the philosopher Kuhn, to describe the point when an existing scientific theory becomes untenable (or at least logically dubious) in the light of new evidence or a more convincing explanation. This leads to a *paradigm shift*.

paradigm shift A dramatic change in an approach to an (academic) subject or problem resulting from a dissatisfaction with the existing theoretical stance. See *Kuhnian revolution* and *paradigm failure*.

paradox (1) An apparently absurd but valid argument or conclusion. (2) An argument which produces contradictory but apparently equally well-reasoned findings. E.g. the famous Ancient

Greek paradox that a Cretan says that 'all Cretans are liars'. If we believe the statement, then we must not believe the speaker, but if we do this, then we must conclude that the statement is true, and if we believe the statement, etc., ad absurdum.

parafovea See *fovea.*

parafoveal benefit The phenomenon whereby items previously only detected in *parafoveal vision* may be processed faster than items not encountered before.

parafoveal vision See *fovea.*

paralexia (1) A misreading of words. (2) A form of *dyslexia* when there is a high frequency of such errors.

parallel distributed processing (PDP) General term for the following model of mental functioning. Processing of information and memory storage takes place using networks of *nodes.* Each node is connected to some, or all, of the other nodes in the same network, and the nodes can *excite* or *inhibit* each other. An item is represented and/or stored as a pattern of excitation of nodes in a network – different items will have different patterns of excitation, but where items have a lot of features in common, then in effect, the items will have similar patterns of excitation. (The situation is akin to a large electronic display made up of a matrix of light bulbs. By having different patterns of lights switched on and off, different pictures can be made). This is known as *distributed representation.* An important feature of PDP is that items can be learnt and recalled without needing a *central controller* to determine whether the correct material has been *encoded*/retrieved. This was needed in many older models, and raised the uncomfortable problem of a *homunculus* in the system. The performance of PDP models also appears to be realistic. For example, if sections of a programme are deliberately rendered inoperative, then the programme often realistically imitates the performance of brain-damaged patients. At a less drastic level, the cell loss experienced in non-dementing ageing in humans has a relatively slight effect (if any at all) on intellectual processes (*graceful degradation*). If this is replicated on a PDP programme by randomly removing a proportion of nodes, then the same phenomenon is observed. Again, the mistakes made by PDP programmes often follow the same patterns as those of human subjects faced with the same task. PDP is very amenable to modelling on the current generation of computers, and has become so intertwined with computing jargon and expertise that all but a gloss of the main findings are beyond the scope of non-specialists. Nonetheless, allowing for the hyperbole of some commentators, the technique is very important, and promises to be one which shapes the next phase of the development of *cognition.* See *auto-association, backward propagation, competitive learning, Hebbian rules, hidden units* and *pattern associator.*

parallel processing See *serial processing.*

parallel scanning Surveying all the items in an array more or less simultaneously. Contrast with *serial scanning.*

parallel search Searching an array by processing several items in the array simultaneously. See *serial search.*

parallel search (memory) Scanning memory for an item by analysing memories of several items simultaneously. See *serial search (memory).*

parallel theory (memory) Theory that a *parallel search* is used to determine whether a newly-presented item is the same as one already stored in memory. See *serial theory (memory)*.

parallel transmission *shingling*.

paramnesia Distorted memory.

paraphasia A profound misuse of words.

parent schema *high level schema*.

parietal lobes The region of the *cerebral cortex* which occupies an area contiguous with an Alice band across the head. Their role is hard to define concisely, but they can be said to be involved in maintaining an awareness of the body's state and location, and in interpreting symbols (e.g. object recognition and some aspects of reading).

paronym A word which sounds like another. Compare with *homophone*.

parsimony principle The general principle that in explaining an experimental finding, the simplest explanation should be preferred.

parsing Breaking an item into smaller constituents (e.g. a sentence into its grammatical structure, a word into its *phonemes*, etc.).

part learning Learning a skill or piece of information in sections. This contrasts with *whole learning*, in which the subject attempts to learn all of the task at once. The relative efficacy of the techniques depends very much on what is being learnt.

partial recall Recalling part of the to-be-remembered item(s). See *tip of the tongue*.

partial report procedure Task in which the subject is told to report only one aspect of a set of stimuli (see e.g. *Sperling's partial report procedure*). See *whole report procedure*.

partially automatic process See *automatic process*.

partist strategy See *wholist strategy*.

PAS *pre-categorical acoustic store.*

passive memory (1) *long-term memory.* (2) Memory for items and events where no conscious effort has been made to remember them. See *active memory*.

passive vocabulary See *active vocabulary*.

pattern associator In some models of *parallel distributed processing*, a mechanism for allowing the association to be made between representations of the same item in different sensory modalities (e.g. the sight and smell of a car exhaust).

pattern masking See *masking*.

pattern masking by noise See *masking*.

pattern masking by structure See *masking*.

pattern recognition Recognition of patterns (i.e. not just geometric patterns, but any groupings of stimuli, such as words, letter, faces, etc.).

PDP *parallel distributed processing.*

peg *conceptual peg.*

peg board task There are several variants of this test of *psychomotor* skill, but the central feature of all of them is that the subject is required to put pegs into holes as quickly as possible.

peg-word system *Elaboration* technique/ mnemonic strategy in which the subject first learns a simple rhyming system (e.g. 'one is a bun; two is a shoe', etc.). The information can then be used in two principal ways. When given a list of numbers to remember, the subject can associate the numbers with their associated images. This enriches the images, and should make them easier to recall. The system can also be used to encode a short series of words. The first word in the list is made into a visual image with the image representing the first number. The same process is repeated for the other words. (e.g. if the first two words in the list of to-be-remembered items are 'clock' and 'car', the subject might form an image of a clock sandwich and a shoe driving a car). See *keyword technique* and *method of loci technique.*

pegword mnemonic *peg-word system.*

pendulum problem *two string problem.*

penetrable system *transparent system.*

percept The image produced by perceptual processes.

perception-based representation See *meaning-based representation.*

perceptron Early *parallel distributed processing* model.

perceptual constancy *perceptual invariance.*

perceptual defence Having a higher *threshold/* slower *reaction time* to respond to an item which is socially or personally embarrassing (e.g. swear words).

perceptual invariance The phenomenon whereby an item is recognized as the same item when viewed from different angles, even though it presents radically different perceptual images. This is a very easy task for humans, but it has so far proved very difficult to programme computers to perform the same task.

perceptual model A mental representation of an event/item.

perceptual selection *selective attention.*

perceptual span The amount of information 'taken in' from the field of view. *Total perceptual span* refers to the area within the field of view from which any information is noted and from which

reasonably detailed information is taken.

performance (linguistics) The utterance of a statement, and by extension, how well the subject performs according to the *syntactic rules* of his/her language.

performance operating characteristic (POC) A graph showing relative performance on two tasks performed simultaneously. Performance on one task is plotted against performance on the other.

Performance scales See *Wechsler Adult Intelligence Scale (WAIS).*

performance test A non verbal test (usually of non verbal intelligence).

peripheral preview A *priming effect,* in which items seen in the periphery of vision (and not consciously processed) are identified faster when the subject focuses on them. The term is particularly used in studies of eye movements in reading.

peripheral process See *central process.*

permanent memory Concept that all memories are stored, and that 'forgotten' memories cannot be retrieved because the right releasing cue has not been used (i.e. that they have not simply been lost from the store).

permastore The concept of a permanent, imperishable memory store.

permission schema Rule of the type that 'x can only be if there is also y'.

perseverations When referring to linguistic errors – the inappropriate repetition of a phrase.

Person Identity Nodes (PINs) See *Interactive Activation and Completion (IAC) network.*

personal equation Adjustment to scores to allow for individual differences in ratings of an item, when attempting to gain an accurate rating of the item (e.g. one might wish to adjust for individual differences in *reaction times* in attempts to time exactly when an event occurred).

PET scan *positron emission tomography.*

Peterson and Peterson task
Brown–Peterson task.

Peterson task *Brown–Peterson task.*

Phoenecian readers and spellers
People who rely heavily on *phonic mediation* in reading and spelling. Compare with *Chinese readers and spellers.*

phone The smallest speech sound which differs from other sounds in all human languages. Note that within a single language, its users may perceive several phones as sounding the same (i.e. they are versions of the same *phoneme*). E.g. the initial sounds of 'kipper' and 'coop' sound identical in English, but they are in fact different phones. By a similar token, several Far Eastern languages regard some 'r' and 'l' sounds as identical (i.e. although they are different phones, they are perceived as a single phoneme). Where two or more *phones* are perceived as the same phoneme within a language, they are known as ***allophones***.

phoneme The smallest unit of speech whose substitution or removal from a word causes a change in the word's sound within the language being spoken. More loosely, the basic sounds which make up words (and even more loosely, the oral equivalent of letters, although do not use this definition within earshot of a linguist). See *phone.*

phoneme restoration effect The phenomenon whereby a pure tone or other non-word sound can be used in lieu of a *phoneme* in a spoken utterance, and this will be unnoticed by the majority of subjects.

phonemic awareness The conscious realization that words are composed of phonemes, and that all words can be constructed from a limited set of phonemes.

phonemic buffer The temporary memory store for *phonemes* in a word retrieved from memory, prior to its pronunciation. Compare with *graphemic buffer.*

phonemic dyslexia *deep dyslexia.*

phonemic output lexicon *Mental lexicon* which stores memories of how to produce spoken letters and letter combinations.

phonemic restoration effect
phoneme restoration effect.

phonemic similarity effect The phenomenon whereby a list of similar sounding words (e.g. cat, rat, bat, hat) is harder to store in *short-term memory* than is a list of dissimilar sounding words (e.g. cat, nag, din, rug).

phonemic word production system
phonemic output lexicon.

phonetic level In a communication, the level of interpretation at which the message's *phonological* content (i.e. how it sounds) is processed.

phonetics See *phonology.*

phonic mediation Pronouncing (usually new or *nonsense*) words by calculating the sound of each letter and stringing the sounds together to form a coherent pronunciation. Compare with *reading by analogy.*

phonological Pertaining to *phonemes.*

phonological coding *Encoding* an item (word, letter, etc.) in terms of its *phonological* structure.

phonological dysgraphia An inability to spell words using *phonological* skills. E.g. patients can spell many real words, but cannot spell *nonsense words* dictated to them. See *phonological dyslexia*.

phonological dyslexia An *acquired dyslexia*—the patient is incapable of reading *nonsense words*, indicating a failure to translate letters into their oral representations.

phonological loop See *articulatory loop* and *working memory*.

phonological priming *Priming* in which the *prime* is a word which contains *phonemes* in common with the *target item*.

phonological recoding *phonological coding*.

phonological similarity effect *phonemic similarity effect*.

phonology (1) The set of *phonemes* used in a particular language. (2) The study of phonemes in terms of their linguistic function. This contrasts with **phonetics**, which is the study of phonemes (particularly, their production and sound characteristics) without regard to their use in language.

phrase-structure grammar An analysis of sentences and other statements into their basic *syntactic* and *semantic* components (verb, adverb, *preposition*, etc.).

physical identity (PI) task See *Posner letter matching task*.

PI *proactive interference*.

PI task *physical identity task*.

Piaget's 'kidnapping' Anecdote of the child psychologist Piaget, which demonstrates the fallibility of *autobiographical memory* and *flashbulb memory*. Piaget had a distinct memory of a kidnap attempt on himself when he was aged 2 years, which his nurse successfully prevented. As an adolescent, Piaget discovered that the nurse had made up the whole episode, and accordingly, his

memory was an elaboration of her story, rather than of a real event.

picture anomalies test Any test in which the subject must identify what is 'wrong' with a series of pictures (e.g. a dog with chicken's legs, a car with square wheels, etc.).

Picture Arrangement Task Sub-test of the *Wechsler* intelligence tests. The subject is shown a set of pictures which must be placed in a sequence so that a cartoon-like story is told.

picture completion task A measure of intelligence. The subject is shown a picture from which something is missing (e.g. a door without a handle). The subject's task is to identify the missing piece. The test can be prone to cultural bias (e.g. showing a picture of the dashboard of a Porsche might not be readily accessible to most of the population).

Picture Producer Memory (PP Memory) Sub-section of the *Script Applier Mechanism*, responsible for providing word meanings.

picture superiority effect The phenomenon whereby, in general, pictures are remembered better than words.

PIM *Predicate Intersection Model*.

PIN *Person Identity Node*.

Platonic form See *prototype*.

plausible retrieval Retrieving an *implicit memory*.

plosive (phonetics) Pertaining to a *phone* whose production involves a temporary build-up of breath, followed by its expulsion (e.g. the first sounds in 'pick' and 'book').

PM *primary memory*.

PMAs *primary mental abilities*.

PMA Test *Primary Mental Abilities Test*.

POC *performance operating characteristic*.

Pollyanna principle The phenomenon whereby items describing pleasant events are better remembered than items describing unpleasant events (named after E.H. Porter's (1868–1920) character 'Pollyanna', an incurable optimist).

pop out Term devised by Treisman to describe the phenomenon whereby, in a *visual search*, if the target is sufficiently distinct from the *distractors*, then it will appear to 'pop out' from the display no matter how many distractors are present.

pop-up The phenomenon of trying to remember something, giving up, and then finding that the memory appears unbidden at a later time.

Porteus mazes A set of paper and pencil mazes, designed to assess *visuo-spatial* intelligence. They are also used to assess patients with some forms of brain damage.

positional bigram frequency See *positional frequency.*

positional frequency The frequency with which a particular section of an item is found in that position. The term is most often used of letters or groups of letters. E.g. the *positional bigram frequency* describes how frequently a particular *bigram* is found in different positions in words (e.g. the bigram 'sk' is found more frequently at the beginning of a word than at the end).

positive feedback See *feedback.*

positive set Group of items to which the subject is instructed to respond positively. Conversely, the subject is instructed to respond negatively to members of the *negative set.* In a *varied set procedure*, membership of the positive and negative sets is changed as the experiment progresses, whilst in a *fixed set procedure*, the membership stays the same.

positive test strategy *confirmation bias.*

positron emission tomography (PET scan) Body scan in which the subject is given a (mildly) radioactive tracer (e.g. injection of radioactive glucose) whose passage in the blood stream is then charted. The PET scan can thus, inter alia, measure: abnormal metabolism, thereby indicating *atrophy* or abnormally functioning cells (e.g. in a tumour); blood flow; energy use by different areas of the brain (and hence observe how areas change activity levels depending upon the psychological task being presented).

Posner letter matching task Task named after its author. There are two principal conditions. In one, the subjects have to judge if pairs of letters, presented one after the other, are physically identical (e.g., 'A-a' and 'B-c' are not physically identical, but 'A-A' or 'a-a' are). This is the *physical identity (PI) task.* In the other (the *name identity (NI) task*), they must judge if pairs of letters, presented one after the other, have the same meaning (e.g. 'A-B' and 'B-c' do not, but 'A-A' and 'A-a' do). Posner et al. found that when the interval between the presentation of the first and second letters was over about 1.5 seconds, then name and physical matches took the same time, but at shorter gaps, the physical match was faster. This implies that the mind identifies physical properties faster than it can access the names of items from *long-term memory.*

post-lexical phonology *addressed phonology.*

post-lexical process Any process which occurs after an item has been identified by the *mental lexicon*.

post-lunch dip See *post-prandial dip*.

post-prandial dip A decline in psychological functioning following consumption of a meal. Since much research has concentrated on the decline following lunch, the term *post-lunch dip* is common.

post-traumatic amnesia (PTA) A period of very dense *amnesia* and confusion in the few hours/days following a serious head injury.

postponement model Model of processing which argues that in *divided attention* tasks, information from one source is 'kept waiting' while information from another source is processed. This contrasts with a *capacity sharing model*, in which it is argued that information from the separate tasks is processed simultaneously.

power law of practice Almost invariably, the speed at which a task is performed improves with practice. If a graph is drawn of speed against a logarithmic scale of the number of practice trials, then a straight line is often found.

power test Any measure in which the accuracy of the answers, rather than the time taken to complete, is of prime importance. This contrasts with the *speed test*, in which the speed at which correct answers can be produced is the principal consideration.

PP Memory *Picture Producer Memory.*

PQ4R method Technique for studying a section of prose (e.g. a textbook chapter). The phrase is an acronym — Preview, Questions, Read, Reflect, Recite, Review.

P.R. Pseudonym of a patient whose symptoms and behaviour were reported in an often-cited case study of *phonological dysgraphia.*

practice distribution *distribution of practice.*

practice, law of *law of practice.*

pragmatic reasoning Reasoning based upon everyday general experience which is characterized by being flexible and applicable across a wide range of situations.

pragmatics The understanding of the intent of an utterance, which may lie beyond a literal interpretation of what has been said or written (e.g. as in euphemisms). See *indirect directive* and *speech acts.*

pragnanz *law of pragnanz.*

pre-attentive processing Analysing items in terms of their features without regard to their whole form. The term is often used of *visual search* tasks, in which the *target item* has features which are different from those of the *distractor items*. Expending *mental effort* on processing the whole image would be wasteful, since the solution can be found simply by looking at the features. The term is also used to describe the relatively crude processing which perceptions are given to decide which will be attended to.

pre-categorical acoustic memory (PAM) Hypothesized very *short-term memory store* which stores auditory information without attempting to identify it. The original argument that the information is not categorized was eventually overturned. The concept/term has been supplanted by that of *echoic memory.*

pre-categorical acoustic store (PAS) *pre-categorical acoustic memory.*

pre-cognitive Pertaining to a function early in a process in which the item being processed has not yet been interpreted or otherwise manipulated by cognitive processes.

pre-cueing *priming*.

pre-lexical phonology *assembled phonology*.

pre-lexical process Any process which occurs before an item has been identified by the *mental lexicon*.

pre-processing Processing which prepares something for a subsequent process. The term may refer to e.g. the mental processing of a perceptual image for subsequent analysis at a more abstract level.

preconscious That which is present but not consciously detected. The term often pertains to processing of information of which the subject is unaware but which can be raised to awareness level.

predicate An assertion about the *subject* of a statement.

predicate calculus A form of logical analysis which contains rules for the representation and analysis of *predicates*.

Predicate Intersection Model (PIM) A *set-theoretic model*, principally concerned with assessing how quickly true/false judgments could be made about statements of the 'all Xs are Y' and 'some Xs are Y' variety.

preferred viewing location (reading) The *fixation position* in reading which the reader usually chooses. This is in contrast with the **convenient viewing location**, which is the fixation point which would yield optimal performance, and which is usually slightly nearer the beginning of the word than the preferred viewing location.

preferred viewing position (reading) *preferred viewing location (reading)*.

preparatory interval See *response signal*.

preposition A word which indicates the relationship between a *noun phrase* and the rest of the sentence. E.g. 'we went TO the zoo', 'I walked UP the stairs', etc.

presentation rate The rate and duration at which items are presented to the subject.

preservation error An error which nonetheless obeys a particular rule followed by the *target* (e.g. misidentifying a word as another real word). This contrasts with a **violation error**, in which the error does not obey a rule obeyed by the target.

prestorage *explicit memory*.

presupposition An assumption which is made during hearing/reading a story/sentence, etc. in order to make sense of it.

preview benefit *priming*.

primacy effect The phenomenon whereby items at the beginning of a list are better remembered than those in the middle. See *serial position effect*.

primal sketch See *Marr's computational theory*.

primary attention Attention directed towards an item because of its intrinsic properties. This contrasts with **secondary attention**, which is attention created by an internal drive, and not because an item is attractive per se.

primary auditory cortex Area of *temporal lobe* responsible for receiving auditory signals. The **secondary auditory cortex** and the **tertiary auditory cortex** are adjacent to the primary area, and are responsible for the interpretation and identification of sounds.

primary component See *serial position effect*.

primary cortex Collective name for areas of *cortex* directly receiving sensory and motor information. The *secondary cortex* refers to areas adjacent to the primary cortex, which integrate and interpret this information. The *tertiary cortex (association cortex)* refers to the remaining cortical areas, which are involved in *cognitive* processes. Note that some commentators group the secondary and tertiary cortices together, and label them the 'association cortex'.

primary memory (PM) (1) *short-term memory*. (2) *short-term store*.

primary mental abilities (PMAs) T h e most basic mental skills, held to underlie all mental processes. Often classified as verbal, numerical, and *visuo-spatial*, but many researchers cite Thurstone's wider calculation of seven primary mental abilities (memory, numerical, perceptual, reasoning, space, verbal, and word fluency). See *Primary Mental Abilities (PMA) Test*.

Primary Mental Abilities (PMA) Test Intelligence test battery assessing ability at Thurstone's seven *primary mental abilities*.

primary task See *secondary task procedure*.

primary visual cortex Area of the *occipital lobe* which receives the direct input from the eyes. The *secondary visual cortex* is principally responsible for interpreting the information received by the primary cortex.

prime See *priming*.

priming (1) Almost always, the term is used synonymously with *congruent priming*, namely, facilitating a *cognitive* process by presenting the subject with information which will help him/her in the task about to be done (the *prime*). Typically, this involves giving the subject a hint about the answer s/he will have to give. E.g. showing the subject the letter 'c' before asking the question, 'what sort of animals do dogs chase?' (see *semantic facilitation*). In *substitution priming*, the prime differs slightly from the *target* (e.g. where the materials are words, the prime might differ from the target by one letter). In *form priming*, the prime resembles the target in general form and appearance. Other prefixes to 'priming' can be used to denote other sources of similarity. These types of priming could all be said to help the subject – i.e. they are all examples of *facilitatory priming*. The reverse is *incongruent priming*, in which the subject receives a prime which does not match up with the target stimulus (e.g. in a letter recognition task, informing the subject that the next letter to appear will have curved lines in it, and then presenting the letter 'X'). This tends to make processing less efficient. (2) The term can also refer to the process of making a subject more sensitive to a particular stimulus.

priming effect An indication that *priming* has occurred. This may refer to a priming experiment in which this was intentional, or to a faulty experimental design where priming has unintentionally occurred, thereby biasing the results.

primitive A basic unit of an item or a process (e.g. *semantic primitive*). The term is also used as an adjective.

primitive action A *semantic primitive* for verbs describing physical action. Schank invented a series of such words. Amongst those often cited by commentators are: **ATRANS** (changing possession); **PTRANS** (physically moving);

MTRANS (providing information about the situation), etc. Other terms ('ingest', 'propel', etc.) roughly maintain their everyday meanings.

primitive feature A very basic feature of a display. E.g., the primitive features of a letter might consist of its lines, curves, the intersection of lines, etc.

principle of a priori plausibility The principle that in processing a statement, the interpretation which accords most with *a priori* reasoning should be accepted.

prior entry *law of prior entry.*

prior knowledge What the subject already knows before the event in question.

proactive inhibition *proactive interference.*

proactive interference (PI) A lowering of *memory span* attributable to having learnt immediately previously several lists of items, often with the added consideration that they are drawn from the same semantic category (e.g. one might have learnt several lists of dog names, and then be given 'collie, daschund, poodle, and sheltie' to remember). *Release from proactive interference* occurs when the subject is required to learn a list drawn from another category (e.g. the subject, after several dog lists, is given a list of flower names). By contrast, *retroactive interference* is the lowering of memory span for early lists caused by interference from lists subsequently learnt.

probe See *probe technique.*

probe detection The ability to detect and act upon the information provided by a *probe.*

probe technique (1) Technique for assessing memory. The subject is given a set of items to remember. S/he is then given a *cue* (a *probe*) about the position of an item in the set, and is asked to produce an appropriate response. E.g. the subject might have been asked to remember a list of words, and when subsequently given one of the words by the experimenter, s/he has to recall which word came next in the list. For another example, see *Sperling's partial report procedure.* (2) The term less commonly refers to a technique in which the subject is asked to perform a task whilst concurrently performing another. The introduction of the second task is called the 'probe'. The technique is used to demonstrate how well the subject can concurrently perform two tasks, and in particular, how performance of the first task is disrupted (e.g. how long the *psychological refractory period* is).

problem isomorphs Problems which, on the surface, appear different, but which have the same underlying structure. An example of problem isomorphs is a *target problem* (the problem currently being faced) and a similarly-structured problem encountered in the past (the *source problem*).

problem memory Memory for a problem. The term is usually used to contrast experts' and novices' memories. E.g. chess experts can more easily memorize the position of the pieces at a stage in a game. However, the information is often very *domain specific* – if the pieces are not presented as they might appear in a real game, then the experts fare little better than the novices.

problem solving by analogy *analogical inference.*

problem-solving set An *Einstellung.* Usually the term is specifically applied to problem solving.

problem space In a problem-solving exercise, the total set of options open to the subject (see *task environment*). The term *basic problem space* refers to all the options available if every permutation of possible actions were attempted. The set of options available at the start of the exercise is called the *initial state*, the set of options once the subject has begun his/her attempt are called the *intermediate states*, and the *goal* is (not surprisingly) called the *goal state*.

procedural knowledge Knowing how to perform a particular act.

procedural learning Learning how to perform a particular procedure (as opposed to learning e.g. a set of facts).

procedural memory Memory of how to perform procedures and actions. See *procedural representation* and *production*, and compare with *episodic memory* and *semantic memory*.

procedural representation A mental representation of how to perform a task. Compare with *analogue representation* and *propositional representation*.

procedural skill The ability to perform a skilful task.

proceduralization (-isation) The transfer in performing a skill from acting on *declarative knowledge* to acting on *procedural knowledge*. This improves efficiency (e.g. in learning to ride a bike, moving from a theoretical knowledge of how to do it to actually doing it).

process deficiency A failure of a mental procedure attributable to an inadequately performed process. See *data-limited process*.

process dissociation procedure Procedure whereby two or more versions of the same task are given, and differences in performance are taken as indicative of differences between the different skills underlying the tasks under comparison.

process model Any model of functioning which represents performance as a series of *processing stages*.

processes, mental *mental processes.*

processing capacity *mental capacity.*

processing load The amount of information which the subject is required to process. This is usually considered in terms of the proportion of his/her *mental capacity* that this will consume.

processing stages In a model of mental processing, the hypothesized different processes by which the mind transforms incoming information into the final desired form.

processing unit A mental component which is responsible for a particular mental act. The term is somewhat interchangeable with *processing stage*.

production In the *ACT* model, a unit of the *procedural memory* store, consisting of a pairing of a 'condition' and an 'action'. The condition is the 'if' clause, the action the 'then' clause, as in 'IF it rains THEN put up your umbrella'. The concept has been used in other models and situations. See *strengthening*.

production deficiency Failure to remember to perform a particular act.

production rule *production.*

production system An *artificial intelligence* programming language, consisting of a set of hierarchically-arranged *productions*, which are conditional commands (e.g. 'if $x = 1$, then y=p', etc.). The programme is used to perform e.g. problem-solving tasks.

productive memory The embellishment of a memory with additional information and suppositions drawn from general knowledge and conjecture.

Professor Aitken One-time mathematics professor at University of Edinburgh, with a prodigious memory for number lists and an ability to perform very complex pieces of mental arithmetic.

programme analogy The use of computer programmes and terms as analogies of psychological functioning.

programme assembly failures Types of *slips of action* in which the subject performs a sequence of actions in an inappropriate combination.

progressive deepening strategy
In problem solving, returning to a smaller range of options than that originally produced, and examining the remaining options in greater depth. This process can be repeated several times, with a smaller number of increasingly deep propositions being produced.

PROLOG *Artificial intelligence* programming language.

pronunciation by analogy
Pronouncing an unfamiliar or new word in a manner akin to one with similar spelling whose pronunciation is already known. See *addressed pronunciation*. This can be an efficient process when all the words with the spelling pattern have the same pronunciation (a **consistent analogy**), but some patterns have varied pronunciations (an **inconsistent analogy**).

proof reading errors In scanning a passage of text for errors, a failure to detect an error. The term usually refers to failure to spot a spelling mistake, but it can also refer to failure to detect faulty grammar, etc. Mistakes in *filler words* are most commonly overlooked, because their high *redundancy* means that less attention is usually paid to them.

proof reading illusion *proof reading error*.

property *feature*.

proposition A statement (usually a simple description or an argument).

proposition, level of *level (of proposition)*.

propositional calculus A form of logic, including a 'grammar' for the construction and analysis of *propositions*.

propositional code *propositional representation*.

propositional content The meaning and/or structure of a statement or argument.

propositional memory Memory of knowledge.

propositional network A representation of a statement in which the connection between its concepts/words is portrayed as a set of interconnecting *nodes* and processes. Shown in diagrammatic form, a statement is often represented as words linked by arrows indicating how one word is related to another. See *semantic network*.

propositional reasoning *conditional reasoning*.

propositional representation See *analogue representation*.

propositionalist argument *propositional representation*.

proprioception Feedback on the body's movements and position.

prosapagnosia A profound failure to recognize faces.

prospective memory The ability to remember to do something in the future. This is contrasted with **retrospective memory** – memory for what has been done in the past.

prospective memory task
Memory measure in which the subject

is required to remember to do something in the future (e.g. to remember to ask the experimenter a particular question when a bell sounds).

protocol (1) A set of instructions. (2) Records of an experiment, observations, etc.

prototype An archetypal member of a category (e.g. in the category of vegetables, 'carrot' is a more likely candidate for prototype than is 'squash'). The prototype need not exist in reality – it can be an amalgam of typical features of members of the category. Such an idealized form is sometimes called a *Platonic form*.

prototype rating A score expressing the level of *prototypicality* an item is felt to possess.

prototype theory The argument that concepts and categories are represented as *prototypes*, rather than lists of attributes.

prototypical case *prototype.*

prototypicality The degree to which an item could be considered a *prototype* of a category.

PRP *psychological refractory period.*

pseudocompound word See *compound word.*

pseudohomophone *Nonsense word* which sounds like a real word when pronounced (e.g. 'phocks').

pseudomorpheme See *compound word.*

pseudoword A *nonsense word* which has a spelling and pronunciation pattern akin to a real word (e.g. 'wabbleburg').

pseudoword advantage The phenomenon whereby, in many instances, *pseudowords* are responded to as quickly as real words relative to random strings of letters.

psychogenic amnesia Disorder in which the patient cannot remember information about a particular period or aspect of his/her life. The information which cannot be recalled often pertains to a particularly stressful or otherwise distressing aspect of the patient's life.

psycholinguistics The study of psychological aspects of language.

psychological refractory period (PRP) See *refractoriness.*

psychological refractory period paradigm *overlapping tasks paradigm.*

psychometrics Strictly speaking, the measurement of psychological traits and skills. Generally used as a synonym of *individual differences.*

psychomotor Pertaining to the mental control of movement, and particularly of voluntary muscles.

psychophysics The study of processing of perceptual stimuli.

PTA *post-traumatic amnesia.*

PTRANS See *primitive action.*

pure artificial intelligence *machine intelligence.*

pursuit eye movement The smooth movement of the eyes when tracking a smoothly-moving object.

pursuit rotor An apparatus consisting of a rotating cylinder on which is printed a target (e.g. a wavy line). The cylinder rotates, and the subject, viewing the cylinder from a fixed position (and often through a slit), perceives the target as moving (e.g. as a continuously undulating line). The subject is required to track the target (e.g. with a pen, stylus, etc.). See *pursuitmeter.*

pursuit tracking See *tracking.*

pursuitmeter Any device for assessing how well a subject can track a moving target. The traditional device for this is the *pursuit rotor*, but more modern devices, using computer generated displays, are likely to eclipse it.

P.V. Neurological patient in an often-cited case study, who had a specific deficit in verbal *short-term memory*.

R

RA *retrograde amnesia.*

RAIP *rapid auditory information processing.*

random dot stereogram An experimental technique devised by Julesz. Subjects are shown two patterns of apparently random black and white shapes (not unlike a television screen when the set is not tuned in), one to either eye. However, when viewed through a stereoscope, the subject perceives a pattern. This is because there is a pattern in the two images, slightly displaced in either of them, and the space around them filled in with random black and white shapes. The shape can only be seen when the information from the eyes is combined in the cortex.

random sentence A collection of words which makes no sense, and has no grammatical structure.

rapid auditory information processing (RAIP) Rather nebulous term for any task in which auditory stimuli are presented at a rapid rate for processing.

rapid serial visual presentation (RSVP) Rapidly presenting visual items for processing/remembering.

rapid visual information processing (RVIP) Rather nebulous term for any task in which visual stimuli are presented at a rapid rate for processing.

rate of forgetting The rate at which items are lost from memory. The phrase typically describes how quickly items from a list are lost from memory over a period of hours or even days and weeks. Typically, there is a large loss in the first hour and a lesser loss over the next day, but thereafter losses are relatively minor (an example of *negatively accelerated change*). Or, in mathematical terms, the amount of information retained is the logarithm of the length of time since it was learnt (the *law of forgetting*). The graph plot of this is, not surprisingly, is known as the *forgetting curve*, and shows a very sharp fall over the first hour or so, and then smooths out.

rationalism The philosophical belief that reason, as opposed to knowledge, (see *empiricism*) is the basis for 'true' knowledge of the existence of items. By extension, the belief that everything can be explained in rational, logical terms, and that the mind and the body are separate entities. See *Descartes' theory of mind* and *empiricism*.

RATN *recursive augmented transition network.*

rats and corn problem See *river crossing problem.*

ray problem Test of problem-solving ability whose basic format was devised by Duncker. Subjects are told of a new type of X-ray which can kill a tumour, but which if given in an intensity strong enough to kill the tumour, will also kill the healthy tissue along the path of the ray. How can the tumour be destroyed? When presented with this information only, few subjects solve the problem. However, if given an analogous story of an army incapable of attacking on one single front because of the terrain, who instead (successfully) attack with several smaller forces from different angles, the subjects' subsequent performances on the ray problem usually improves dramatically. This is an example of *analogical inference*.

R.E. Subject in an often-cited case study with an apparently congenital condition akin to *phonological dyslexia* (she had severe problems with processing phonological information).

reaction time (RT) The time taken for a person to respond to the appearance of a stimulus. A *simple reaction time (SRT)* is the time taken for a subject to respond when there is only one type of stimulus and one type of response. A *choice reaction time (CRT)* is the time taken for a subject to make the correct response to a stimulus, when there is more than one stimulus, and each stimulus requires a different response. Reaction time tasks can also be presented at two rates. In *serial reaction time (SRT)* tasks, the subject is presented with successive stimuli to respond to without a time gap between them. In *discrete reaction time (DRT)* tasks, there is a delay between successive presentations, often with a prompt to prepare the subject. The above terms can be combined: *SSRT – serial simple reaction time; DSRT – discrete simple reaction time; SCRT – serial choice reaction time; DCRT – discrete choice reaction time*. The *speed-error tradeoff function* measures the degree to which an individual is prepared to 'trade' speed at performing a choice reaction time task (i.e. slow down) in order to reduce the number of errors made. Reaction time measures are used frequently in experimental psychology, because they give a measure of the efficiency with which a mental process occurs, and by manipulating the information being processed, and comparing the speed with which it is processed, an indication of how the underlying mental procedures operate can be gleaned. In addition, the reaction time is very well correlated with *fluid intelligence*, indicating that both are measures of neural processing efficiency.

reactivation (memory) The ease with which a memory can be recalled. This is largely determined by its *strength*.

readability Any measure of the ease with which a passage of text can be read. Typically, a mathematical formula (for the mathematically minded, a regression equation) derived from characteristics of a sample of the text in question is used. Usually, readability is expressed in terms of the minimum age at which an average person could read the text in question.

reading by analogy Pronouncing (usually new or *nonsense*) words in a similar manner to words which look similar (e.g. pronouncing 'zant' to rhyme with 'pant'). Compare with *phonic mediation*.

reading by ear *phonic mediation*.

reading by phonological buildup *phonic mediation*.

realistic language comprehension (RLC) Property of an *artificial intelligence* comprehension programme which can quickly interpret normal pieces of prose.

reality monitoring Distinguishing between memories of events which really happened (*externally derived memories*) and those which were only imagined (*internally derived memories*). Generally, the subject's ability to separate the real from the imagined is less for old than for recent memories – see *War of the Ghosts*.

recall The process of retrieving a memory without any *cues* or other aids. Contrast with *cued recall* and *recognition*.

recall task Memory measure in which the subject must attempt to remember a set of items purely from memory (contrast with *recognition task*). In a **cued recall task**, the experimenter provides the subject with a prompt (e.g. the first letter of a to-be-remembered word).

Received Pronunciation (RP) The pronunciation of Standard English – i.e. the most socially 'correct' pronunciation of British English.

receiver operating characteristic curve (ROC curve) A graph plotting the probability of a *hit* against the probability of a *false alarm*. Often, a line of forty-five degrees is drawn from the zero of the graph. This shows what a subject's ROC curve would look like if s/he were randomly responding. The further the subject's line is to the left of this line, the better his/her performance. The information gained from the ROC curve is used in *signal detection analysis*.

recency component See *serial position effect*.

recency effect The phenomenon that items at the end of a list are better remembered than those in the middle. See *serial position effect*.

recency judgement Judging how recently an event occurred. In some memory experiments, this may be assessed by asking the subject to judge which of two items in a previously presented list occurred more recently.

reception paradigm Experimental technique used to assess *concept formation* abilities. The subject is shown items one at a time, and on each occasion must judge if an item is an example of the category. The subject does not know the rules governing the category – the aim of the experiment is for the subject to uncover the rules. After each judgment, the subject is told whether s/he is correct. This enables the subject to revise his/her strategy accordingly (see *wholist strategy*).

receptive aphasia See *aphasia*.

recipient case See *case grammar*.

recognition The process of identifying a currently-presented item or event as one which has been encountered on a previous occasion. Some commentators distinguish between recognition and *identification*, where 'identification' is the recognition of an item which can also be named, whilst 'recognition' refers to being able to identify an item but being unable to name it. Contrast with *recall*.

recognition confusion Mistakenly recognizing a (usually similar) item as a to-be-remembered item.

recognition failure Failing to recognize items which are subsequently recalled in a test of the same set of items.

recognition task Memory measure in which the subject is required to decide if a presented item has been encountered before (e.g. in 'real life' if the test is a measure of ability to recognize famous faces; or earlier in the experiment if the set of to-be-remembered items has been devised by the experimenter). In a **forced choice recognition task** (**alternative forced choice task (AFC)**) the subject is presented with an item s/he has encountered before, together with *distractors* – the task is to choose between them. The number of choices is sometimes denoted in the title of the task – **2AFC** denotes two choices, '3AFC' three choices, etc. Contrast with *recall task*.

recognition unit A (real or hypothesized) unit in the brain which only responds to one type of stimulus. E.g. there are cells in the monkey *cortex* which only respond when the monkey is looking at a face.

recollection General term for recall of *long-term memories*. The term often is used to describe recall of *autobiographical memories*, and carries the implication that the subject might have actively to piece together information, rather than simply automatically producing the entire memory 'in one go'.

reconstruction method Method of *cueing* in which the subject is presented with some of the features of the *to-be-remembered* item.

recovered memory Recovery of a suppressed memory by means of hypnosis, drugs, or other therapeutic methods. The phenomenon has gained media notoriety because it has been alleged that many recovered memories of e.g. being the victim of child abuse may be *false memories* triggered by suggestions (unwitting or otherwise) by therapists – the ***false memory syndrome***.

recurrent lateral inhibition See *lateral inhibition*.

recurring items test Any test of memory in which a subject is presented with a series of items, and must indicate when s/he detects a repetition.

recursive augmented transition network (RATN) *Augmented transition network* in which the programme can also re-apply the routines already being run to analyse embedded clauses within a statement.

reduction coding A *mnemonic* technique in which the subject attempts to minimize the amount of information s/he has to memorize by encoding only the key features of the to-be-remembered items. This is a common method of exam revision, in which students remember a series of sentences written in extreme shorthand which capture the essence of the material they are revising. A similar technique is the *acronym technique*.

reductionism The belief that the 'mind' is solely a production of the physical activity of the brain, and that accordingly, all psychological acts can ultimately be explained in physical terms.

reductive inference Inference made about a lengthy communication in order to extract its essence.

redundancy The phenomenon whereby a proportion of information is extraneous to the needs of adequate comprehension. E.g. studies of eye movements in reading show that many *filler words* are skipped over (i.e. never read), yet the subject can still comprehend the text. However, supposedly redundant information does have its uses. Extra information about an item can make it more memorable (see *levels of processing*) and/or more interesting (e.g. the plot of a Shakespearean play can be summarized in a couple of paragraphs – however, it is the beauty of the 'redundant' descriptive language which is one of its chief glories).

reference signal See *feedback signal*.

refractoriness The state of a subject who must make two responses. There is usually a delay between making the first response and starting the second, whose length (the ***psychological refractory period***) depends upon the processing demands involved.

refractory state A state in which a process is incapable of responding, because it is recovering from previous activity.

regression (reading) The movement of the eye backwards to a section of text already read.

regular spelling Spelling which is 'logical' (i.e. possesses **spelling-to-sound regularity**) such as 'bat'. This contrasts with an **irregular spelling**, which is 'illogical' (e.g. 'quay'). See *consistency (spelling)* and *orthographic regularity*.

regularity effect Phenomenon whereby words with a *regular spelling* are pronounced with a faster *latency* than words with an *irregular spelling*. See *consistency effect*.

rehearsal (memory) The process of repeating to-be-remembered items 'in the head' in an effort to remember them better. This can be categorized into two kinds – *maintenance rehearsal* simply rehearses the information without attempting to transform it, or add properties to it which will make it more memorable. *Elaborative rehearsal* is synonymous with *elaboration*.

related items Items which are related according to a system specified by the experimenter (e.g. the relationship between a *prime* and a *target*). By the same reasoning, **unrelated items** are not related according to the specified system.

relational concept See *object concept*.

relational inference *syllogism*.

relearning method *savings method*.

release from proactive interference See *proactive interference*.

reminiscence peak The phenomenon whereby the bulk of *autobiographical memories* stem from the period between 10 and 30 years of age.

remote memory Memory for non-autobiographical events which have occurred during a subject's lifetime. A frequent proviso is that these events must not include very famous ones, which are seen as part of common general knowledge, and thus more properly classified as part of *semantic memory*.

repetition errors Types of *slip of action* where the person erroneously repeats the same stage in a process (e.g. polishing the same ornament twice when dusting).

repetition priming Identifying or perceiving an item faster because it has been encountered before.

repisodic memory *generic memory*.

representation problem The problems associated with creating a mental representation of a problem or situation in such a manner that it can be comfortably processed by the subject.

representations See *Marr's computational theory.*.

representative heuristic The phenomenon whereby subjects tend to categorize items according to how closely they fit preconceived ideas of what the items are usually like.

representativeness heuristic *representative heuristic*.

repression The unconscious prevention, diminution, or retardation of recognizing and/or recalling items which are embarrassing or otherwise emotionally painful. Contrast with *suppression*.

reproductive memory Memory for information which preserves the meaning of the original material, but not in precisely its original format (e.g. in describing the plot of a play, one would recall the gist of the story, and perhaps a few of the more memorable lines, but one would not attempt to reproduce the whole of the script). See *verbatim memory*.

reproductive thought Thought which repeats pre-existing thoughts, stereotypes, etc.

Rescorla-Wagner rule A method of *backward propagation*.

residual ability Skills which are retained by neurological patients.

resource allocation See *central processor*.

resource-limited process Mental process which may fail, or fail to operate at the optimum level, because its demands exceed the available *mental capacity*. The high demand can be because e.g. the skill is relatively unpractised and/or because it is inherently difficult. Contrast with *data-limited process*.

response buffer A *buffer* responsible for temporary storage of information to be used in providing a response. In some instances, this is synonymous with a *phonemic buffer*.

response competition The process of deciding which response to select.

response criterion (β) See *signal detection analysis*.

response modality The manner in which the subject must make his/her response (e.g. written, spoken, button pressing, etc.).

response signal A signal indicating that the subject must provide a response. Typically, the subject has been given an item to process, and the response signal is a request for them to reveal the results of their thinking. The response signal may be preceded by a *warning signal,* and the gap between the warning and response signals is called the ***preparatory interval***.

response-signal technique Experimental method in which the subject is presented with a stimulus, and then must make a response to the stimulus when a signal is provided. By varying the interval between the stimulus and the signal, the experimenter can control the amount of processing the subject can do before being required to make a response.

response-stimulus interval (RSI) The gap between the subject making a response and the presentation of the next stimulus in a *reaction time* experiment.

response time *reaction time.*

response-to-next stimulus interval *response-stimulus interval.*

resting level of activation See *level of activation*.

retroactive priming Improved recognition/processing of items encountered earlier caused by encountering later items.

restructuring Radically altering the structure of a *schema* to incorporate new information. Compare with *accretion* and *tuning*.

retention process A mental process which maintains information in a memory store.

retinal image A visual image as it arrives at the retina (i.e. prior to any neural processing).

retrieval The process of retrieving a memory so that it can be consciously examined.

retrieval cue *cue*, definition (1).

retrieval practice effect *spacing effect.*

retroactive inhibition *retroactive interference.*

retroactive interference (RI) See *proactive interference*.

retrograde amnesia (RA) See *amnesia*.

retrospective memory See *prospective memory*.

reverse mapping (RM) See *consistent mapping*.

rewrite rule (linguistics) A rule stating how a sentence/phrase can be represented symbolically.

Rey-Osterreith figure A complex geometric drawing which subjects are required to copy from sight, and then later to copy from memory.

R.G. Pseudonym of the patient whose symptoms and behaviour were reported in an often-cited case study of *phonological dyslexia* and *surface dysgraphia*.

RI *retroactive interference*.

Ribot's hypothesis The theory that in damaged or decaying minds, memories for recent events will be worse than memories for remote ones.

right-headed word *Compound word* whose *root morpheme* is at the end (e.g. 'illogical'). Logically enough, a **left-headed word** has its root morpheme at the beginning.

rime See *syllable*.

river crossing problem A genre of problem used in studies of problem-solving ability. The subject is told that a certain number of X and a certain number of Y must be transported across a river in a boat which can only carry a small number of passengers at one time. Since X and Y are incompatible (e.g. *detectives and criminals, foxes and geese, missionaries and cannibals, orcs and hobbits, wolves and sheep, rats and corn*, psychologists and sociologists, etc.) the more vulnerable of the two must never be outnumbered, either in the boat or on the shore. The subject must arrange a transportation schedule to fit these requirements.

Rivermead Behavioural Memory Test A battery of memory tasks analogous to everyday situations where memory is required (e.g. face recognition, *prospective memory* tasks, remembering a route set out by the experimenter, etc.). The test is intended for adults of all ages with memory problems, and it is often used for assessing demented patients. A children's version is also available.

RLC *realistic language comprehension*.

RM *reverse mapping*.

ROC curve *receiver operating characteristic curve*.

root morpheme *Morpheme* which is in itself a word (e.g. 'legible' in 'illegible').

rotation heuristic Phenomenon whereby people tend to treat visual displays as more oriented towards a horizontal or vertical axis than they actually are.

RP *Received Pronunciation*.

RSI *response-stimulus interval*.

RSVP *rapid serial visual presentation*.

RT *reaction time*.

rule discovery task Task in which subjects must uncover the rule underlying a phenomenon set by the experimenter.

running memory span *dynamic memory span*.

RVIP *rapid visual information processing*.

S

S (1) In linguistics, shorthand for a sentence. (2) The pseudonym of an exceptionally good mnemonist studied by Luria. (3) The pseudonym of a neurological patient in an often-cited case study, with visual *agnosia*. (4) Abbreviation of 'experimental subject'.

S-R learning *stimulus-response learning.*

saccade A rapid eye movement from one fixation point to another. The term is often used in describing a subject viewing a stationary visual display, and especially in reading. See *pursuit eye movement.*

saccadic Pertaining to *saccade*.

saccadic movement *saccade.*

saccadic suppression The phenomenon whereby during a *saccade*, nothing (or virtually nothing) is perceived.

SAM *Script Applier Mechanism.*

SAM task *search and memory task.*

same-different experiment Any experimental method in which the subject is presented with pairs of items and must judge if they are the same or different. One of the most frequent uses of this method is in assessing the degree of difference which must exist between objects for the difference to be noted (e.g. two very slightly different shades of the same colour).

same-opposite test *synonym-antonym test.*

Sapir-Whorf hypothesis *linguistic relativity hypothesis.*

Sarah Chimpanzee taught to use 'language' involving placing plastic symbols on a board. The general comments on *Washoe's* language use apply here also, although overall, Sarah's linguistic skills seem to be rather more complex than Washoe's.

SAS model The 'SAS' stands for **supervisory activating system**, a mechanism for controlling actions. The SAS mechanism is capable of 'interfering' with an ongoing activity, biasing it towards particular movements, etc.

savings method Any experimental technique in which learning/memory is assessed by how much faster a subject performs a task/learns a set of items when he or she has done it before.

schadenfreude Pleasure at another's misfortune.

schema See *schema theory.*

schema-driven error Error caused by trying to fulfil the expectations of a *schema* when the response is inappropriate (e.g. recalling seeing waiters in bow ties in a restaurant when there were none, because one's 'restaurant schema' has a *default value* of bow-tied waiters).

schema plus correction Bartlett's term for a *schema* which describes the majority of cases of a given situation, with an additional collection of exceptions. E.g. one might have a schema for how to deal with one's relatives but have an additional set of concepts which are only used for one exceptionally cantankerous uncle.

schema plus tag Adaptation of *schema theory* which argues that memory of an event is a combination of the generic memories of the appropriate *schemas,* plus a collection of any exceptional incidents (e.g. memory of a visit to a restaurant may be of a conventional dining experience, plus additional 'tags' of unusual decor, an objectionable diner at an adjacent table, etc.).

schema theory Theory first proposed by Bartlett, who, in a series of elegant experiments, demonstrated that memories and perceptions are shaped by prior expectations. A set of prior expectations on a particular topic is called a *schema*. E.g. if we were trying to remember a trip to a new restaurant, we already have a schema for what a restaurant visit is like. Accordingly, remembering is made easier because we have a plan which we can relate things to. Memorization would be much harder if we had to remember everything 'from scratch' (e.g. the concept of waiter service, of ordering from a menu, etc.). Similarly, a schema can make perception of an event easier. E.g. if we were to describe the restaurant visit to someone, then their restaurant schema will enable them to understand the description more easily. The schema is normally very useful, although it can produce problems if the event does not correspond to an existing schema. Either little is remembered (because no sense can be made of it), or the information is biased, to make it fit an existing schema (see *War of the Ghosts*). A **high level schema** refers to a schema which may contain several smaller schemas, which are called **low level schemas**. E.g. a 'going on holiday' schema might contain, inter alia, 'packing bags' and 'checking into hotels' schemas. The schema theory is widely accepted in principle, although how it works is still open to debate.

schemas Plural of *schema*. *Schemata* is also acceptable.

schemata Plural of *schema*. *Schemas* is also acceptable.

scientific method A rather nebulous term. Several commentators define it as the examination of a phenomenon by observation, inference, and verification. In addition, there is an implication that an objective measure is being taken, not based upon subjective opinions. However, philosophers of science would dispute whether there can ever be true objectivity in observation, and, inter alia, arguments that science has taken an essentially 'masculine' approach have been advanced. For the interested reader, there is a large and increasingly tedious literature on the subject.

script A *schema* for an event or action (e.g. paying for goods or services, etc.). Compare with *frame* and *memory organization packet*.

Script Applier Mechanism (SAM) Artificial intelligence programme which interpreted stories through a variety of *scripts* which had been provided.

script-irrelevant action Action which one would not expect to find in the *script* in question (e.g. kicking a football in a paying for goods or services script). Compare with *script-relevant action*.

script-relevant action Action which one would expect to find in the *script* in question (e.g. signing a cheque in a paying for goods or services script). Compare with *script-irrelevant action*.

SCRT *serial choice reaction time*.

search and memory (SAM) task Task in which the subject must search an array of items for a *target* or set of targets. A memory load is imposed, since the subjects are required to remember the identities of the targets (by varying the set, the memory load is altered). The identity of the targets can be changed or can remain the same as the test progresses.

search graph A diagrammatic representation of the range of options available to a subject at different stages in a problem-solving task. Since only one or a limited set of choices will yield the correct option, it is possible to see how far an erroneous response veers away from the correct one.

search tree *search graph.*

second order isomorphism See *isomorphism.*

secondary attention See *primary attention.*

secondary auditory cortex See *primary auditory cortex.*

secondary cortex See *primary cortex.*

secondary memory *long-term memory.*

secondary recall cue A recalled item which acts as a cue to recalling other items.

secondary task procedure Experimental technique in which the subject, in addition to performing a task assessing the skill in which the experimenter is most centrally interested (the **primary task**), performs a second task. This usually has the aim of lowering performance on the primary task. By varying the nature of the secondary task, primary task performance can be altered by varying amounts, and this can yield information on the structure of the primary task. E.g. if a subject is performing primary task X, and a secondary task requiring verbal skills has little effect on X, but a secondary *visuo-spatial* task does, then we can conclude that X is probably very reliant on visuo-spatial skills. There is a wide variety of permu-

tations of this technique. In most instances, performance on the secondary task is of marginal interest, although in some cases, the level of performance may be used as a measure of how much *mental capacity* the subject has left after the primary task has exacted its share.

secondary visual cortex See *primary visual cortex.*

segment When used as a verb, refers to mentally breaking an item into smaller units (e.g. a word into its constituent *phonemes*).

segment and label *bottom-up processing.*

selection mechanism The mental process which enables *selective attention* to take place.

selection restriction A mechanism in a model of mental functioning which limits the choice of alternatives. This is often done to speed up processing. E.g. if in chess, all possible permutations of two or more moves ahead were considered before making a move, then a chess game would take a ridiculously long time. Clearly, there must be a mechanism to restrict moves to a sensible smaller set of alternatives.

selective attention The ability to concentrate on one aspect of a *sensory input* to the exclusion of other aspects of it and other inputs.

selective combination See *selective encoding.*

selective comparison See *selective encoding.*

selective encoding Processing only certain aspects of an event (e.g. a problem). This can be efficient, provided the relevant aspects are selected. A related concept is the **selective combination**, in which the solution is only apparent when certain pieces of information are combined. If the information must be combined with previously-learnt information, then this is known as *selective comparison*.

selective filter *selection mechanism.*

selective listening task *split span procedure.*

self schema A *schema* of one's personal details and sense of self.

self-awareness The awareness of oneself as a cognitive being. See *Descartes' theory of mind.*

self-reference effect (1) The phenomenon whereby items are typically easier to process and/or remember if they are perceived as referring to oneself. (2) Some commentators use the term synonymously with the *medical student effect.*

self-terminating search *self-terminating serial scanning.*

self-terminating serial scanning See *serial scanning.*

semantic Pertaining to the meaning of a word or statement.

semantic activation (SA) *Activation* (definition 2 or 3) of a process concerned with the identification of a *semantic* attribute of an item.

semantic analysis Analysing an item for meaning.

semantic coding *Encoding* an item in terms of its meaning.

semantic confusion Erroneously perceiving/remembering a word or other item which is similar in meaning to the intended word/item.

semantic decomposition Breaking down a statement into its semantic components (i.e. down to the level of its *semantic primitives*).

semantic distance effect Phenomenon whereby, when asked to provide examples of a category, *prototypes* are more likely to be produced than less typical examples.

semantic dyslexia *surface dyslexia.*

semantic error Misperceiving a word for one of similar meaning (e.g. reading 'cabbage' as 'cauliflower').

semantic facilitation *Priming* by a *semantic* link between the items in question. E.g., a word is recognized faster if a semantically related word has preceded it (e.g. 'butter' will be recognized faster when the subject has just seen 'bread' than if s/he has just seen 'tango').

semantic feature A property of an item which is a necessary part of its basic definition (e.g. 'mammal' is a defining feature of 'dog').

semantic feature model A *network model* in which associations between items are determined in terms of their attributes.

semantic inhibition *Inhibition* (definition 2) caused by an item which is *semantically* related to the item whose processing has been suppressed.

Semantic Information Units (SIUs) See *Interactive Activation and Completion (IAC) network.*

semantic marker *semantic feature.*

semantic memory (1) Tulving's term for memory for facts not directly concerned with one's own life. This is contrasted with *episodic memory*, which is memory for events directly concerned with one's own life (e.g. personal details, day-to-day occurrences, etc.). (2) Memory for word meanings.

semantic network A model of how we represent connections in meaning between different items (the type of link can be of several kinds – e.g. the items belong to the same category, are used in the same activity, are opposites, etc.). The model has many formats, but all or most are based on computer modelling, and assume that individual items are represented by *nodes*. Nodes representing related items are linked to each other. The closer the relationship, the stronger the link. The strength of a connection is expressed in several ways. One of the most common is to envisage that when one node is excited, it sends excitatory signals to the nodes it is connected to. The stronger the connection, the greater the excitatory signal. E.g. if A is connected strongly to B but only weakly to C, then exciting A will lead to a considerable rise in the excitation of B, but only mild excitation of C. In addition, the model assumes that frequently associating two nodes together will lead to a strengthening of the link. The semantic network models can explain several aspects of semantic processing, including *semantic facilitation*. See *propositional network* and *spreading activation*.

semantic priming *semantic facilitation.*

semantic primitive A word of very basic meaning forming the basis of an absolute core vocabulary. In some linguistic studies, words are 'decomposed' into their semantic primitives. E.g. the word 'man' might be decomposed into 'adult' and 'male'.

semantic representation The mental representation of items in terms of their meaning and uses.

semantic substitution error *substitution error.*

semantic system General term for any model of how *semantic* information is processed. In some models of auditory processing, it is the process responsible

for identifying the meanings of items from their sound structure by the *auditory lexicon*, which in turn accesses the semantic system to generate their meaning.

semantic violation See *syntactic violation.*

semanticity The ability of a language to describe.

semantics (1) The meaning conveyed by a statement or phrase. (2) The study of the same.

semasiography Writing system in which words and concepts are represented by signs (often literal pictorial representations). This is one of the earliest forms of writing, and semasiographies are the ancestors of *logographic* writing systems.

sememe *semantic primitive.*

semiotics The study of signs and communication.

sensitivity (signal detection theory) See *signal detection analysis.*

sensorimotor aphasia *global aphasia.*

sensory aphasia *Wernicke's aphasia.*

sensory buffer *iconic memory.*

sensory information store (SIS) *sensory register.*

sensory input Any information obtained from the senses. There is the implication that the information is in a 'raw' state – i.e., it has not yet been interpreted beyond any 'refinements' created by perceptual processing.

sensory memory *sensory register.*

sensory register A very short-term store of the *sensory input*. Examples include *echoic memory* and *iconic memory.*

sentence completion test Any test in which the subject is required to complete unfinished sentences. The procedure can be used in a manner similar to the *cloze procedure*, to test linguistic skills.

sentence context A *contextual effect* in which the preceding words in a sentence affect the speed of recognition of the next word(s).

sentence family Sentences, which although differing in *surface structure*, possess the same *deep structure*. E.g. 'the boy kicked the ball', and 'the ball was kicked by the boy' have a different surface appearance, but mean the same thing.

sentence-picture verification task Experimental procedure in which the subject must decide if a picture is an accurate representation of a sentence (the term often refers to a task in which the sentence and picture portray an arrangement of shapes – e.g. 'the square is above the triangle').

sentence span (1) The amount of information retained about earlier sections of a passage of prose which a subject can remember and use in comprehending later sections of the same passage (e.g. to interpret an *anaphoric reference*). (2) The maximum sentence length which a person can remember.

sentence verification The process of deciding that a sentence 'makes sense'. Depending upon the situation, this may be determining that it expresses a truth, is grammatically correct (regardless of meaning – e.g. 'cats can talk'), etc.

sentence verification technique Presenting a subject with the task of performing *sentence verification* (typically, the subject must decide if a statement is true or false).

sentential grouping A (usually) inefficient and illogical classification of objects on the basis that they can be included in the same sentence or short story.

separable attribute See *integral attribute*.

serial choice reaction time (SCRT) See *reaction time*.

serial exhaustive search Searching all the contents of a memory/a display one at a time, before making a decision. See *serial scanning*.

serial learning Learning a list of items in the same order as they are presented. Contrast with *serial recall*.

serial ordering Placing the stages of a complex process in their correct order.

serial position curve A record of how well the items in a *serial learning* or *serial recall task* are remembered (i.e. how well the item in each position in the list is remembered).

serial position effect The phenomenon whereby items at the beginning (the ***primary component***) and end of a list (the ***recency component***) of to-be-remembered items are remembered better than those in the middle. See *primacy effect* and *recency effect*.

serial processing Processing of information by *processing stages*, in which a stage has to be completed before processing by another stage can begin. This contrasts with ***parallel processing***, in which several processes can be carried out simultaneously.

serial reaction time (SRT) See *reaction time*.

serial recall Attempting to *recall* as many items as possible, in the order in which they were originally presented. This contrasts with *serial learning*, in which the list is learnt. See *free recall*.

serial scanning Scanning an array of items one item at a time. Usually the term is synonymous with ***self-terminating serial scanning***, in which the subject only searches until the *target* item is found. Hence, the more items in the display, the longer on average it should take the subject to find the target item. (Technical note: generally, the slope of the curve for finding a target item is about half the slope where there is no target and the subject makes a correct 'no' response). *Exhaustive serial scanning* involves examining all items before a response is made, regardless of when the target item is found. The degree to which subjects adopt a serial scanning technique, as opposed to a *parallel scanning* technique, is debatable.

serial search *serial scanning* or *serial search (memory)*.

serial search (memory) Scanning memory for an item by examining one 'area' of memories at a time. See *parallel search*.

serial self-terminating search *self-terminating serial scanning*.

serial simple reaction time (SSRT) See *reaction time*.

serial theory (memory) Theory that a *serial search* is used to determine if a newly-presented item is the same as one already stored in memory. See *parallel theory (memory)*.

series continuation problem *continuation problem*.

servomechanism Any process in which a movement or other act is monitored by attending to *feedback*, and adjustments made based on this. This is sometimes contrasted with *ballistic movement*.

set effect The manner in which prior experience of a type of problem biases performance on subsequent similar problems.

set inference *Inference* of properties of an item based on the properties of the rest of its set's members (e.g. Ford is a brand of car; as all other cars have wheels, it may be assumed that the Ford has wheels).

set-theoretic model Model of mental functioning exploring how an item's membership of a set can be verified or refuted.

S.F. Pseudonym of a subject in an often-cited study, who was trained to memorize prodigiously long sequences of numbers.

shadowing Experimental method in which the subject is required to 'shadow' a piece of speech by repeating it as s/he is hearing it spoken. The technique is used in some measures of *selective attention*.

shallow In cognition, the term usually refers to the surface structure of an item or situation. E.g. *shallow processing* is the processing of information about the surface of an item or situation. E.g. the shallow processing of a word might attend to what it sounds like, or how long it is, but little more. The term is not synonymous with 'trivial' or 'worthless'. See *deep*.

shallow processing See *shallow*.

sharpening In recalling a story, lengthy piece of prose, etc., exaggerating an important piece of information.

Shass Pollack A Jewish scholar who has attained the remarkable feat of memorizing the whole of the Talmud (the sacred Jewish text), not only in terms of its words, but also the visual appearance of the pages (i.e. the spatial location of the words – this is feasible because the typographical layout is identical for all editions of the Talmud).

Shepard and Teightsoonian recognition paradigm Measure of recognition skills devised by the aforementioned authors. Subjects are presented with a list of items, and have to indicate if an item makes a repeated appearance. The items are arranged so that they repeat themselves at different interval lengths (i.e. some items repeat immediately or almost immediately, whilst some do not reappear until a considerable number of intervening items have been displayed).

Shepard mental rotation task *Mental rotation task* devised by Shepard and colleagues. In one 'basic' version of the task, subjects are shown two three-dimensional shapes, which are shown in different orientations. Subjects are required to judge if they are identical in shape. It has been found that where the shapes are identical, the time taken to judge this is proportional to the number of degrees through which the image has to be rotated.

Sherman See *Lana*.

shingling The phenomenon whereby the sound of phonemes in a spoken word overlap with each other (e.g. in speaking the word 'cat', there is no clear acoustic gap between the 'c', 'a', and 't' sounds).

short-term auditory store (STAS) *echoic memory*.

short-term memory (STM) (1) A memory store which can hold a limited amount of information for a short period. (2) The processes involved in this storage. Figures for the amount of information the store can hold vary between individuals and situations. A number typically quoted is '7 ± 2', after a famous paper by Miller (see *Magical Number Seven*). What constitutes a 'short period' is also variable, with figures from two seconds to a minute or so being cited by different authors. Functionally, the STM is the store into which new information is placed after being processed through the *sensory register* (the

store may also be used as a repository for information retrieved from *long-term memory (LTM)*). The degree to which STM differs from long-term memory has been debated at very great length. The two stores are linked to different anatomical structures, and in most cases (although not exclusively) information passes through the STM store before being transferred to long-term memory. As a general rule, storage and retrieval from STM is easily disrupted (e.g. *phonemic similarity effect*), whilst long-term memory is felt to be more robust (although again, this has been debated). However, note that STM must use information supplied by long-term memory (e.g. in remembering lists of words – how can the words be recognized without reference to the vocabulary stored in LTM?). This has led some commentators to argue for a more precise terminology – see *short-term store*. Also note that STM can apply to any sensory modality – i.e. there is an STM for touch, vision, hearing, etc. See *working memory*.

short-term sensory store (STSS) *iconic memory* and/or *echoic memory*.

short-term span See *span*.

short-term store (STS) (1) Most often used as a synonym for *short-term memory*. (2) However, note that the term is used by some researchers to denote only those mental mechanisms involved in memorizing items in a short-term store. They use the term 'short-term memory' for the process of short-term memorization as it occurs in practice. E.g. suppose a subject is asked to remember 'cat, rat, bat, mat' in a short-term memory experiment. The subject will know what the to-be-remembered words mean, and s/he can only do this by referring to his/her vocabulary store in *long-term memory (LTM)*. In other words, the memorization process does not purely involve a short-term store – other memory processes are also used. Hence the need for a term denoting the processes unique to short-term memorization. By the same token, researchers sometimes create a distinction between long-term memory and **long-term store (LTS)**, where the latter refers purely to the process of storing long-term information, and not to the additional short-term memory processes used in storing and retrieving it (which would, however, be included in the wider definition of 'long-term memory').

short-term visual store (STVS) *iconic memory*.

SHRDLU *Artificial intelligence* programme by Winograd. The programme consists of a 'computer game' in which a number of coloured blocks can be moved by suitable requests to the programme. SHRDLU could not only obey requests in conventional English (with a vocabulary restricted to the immediate situation), but also could explain why it had performed previous actions, and the reasons for its current activity.

sight vocabulary (reading) *visual word recognition system*.

signal detection analysis A method of determining how accurately a subject can discriminate between a signal and *noise*. The theory supposes that the subject, upon detecting any stimulus, will decide that it is either a signal or merely background noise (e.g. like listening for a faint morse code broadcast against a background of static hiss). Strong signals will be readily recognized as signals, but weaker signals may be less easily detected, and may be confused with noise. Conversely, strong noise may be erroneously identified as a signal. From this, it can be extrapolated that the subject can make four types of response: *true positive* (correctly identifying a signal as a signal, also known as a *hit*); *true negative* (correctly rejecting noise, because it is not a signal); *false positive* (incorrectly identifying noise as a signal, also known as a *false alarm*); and *false negative* (incorrectly rejecting a signal because it is misidentified as noise). A subject who only ever makes true positive and true negative responses has a perfectly operating system. However, if the subject makes an appreciable number of false responses, then his/her perceptions are faulty. The greater the accuracy, the greater the **sensitivity** of the subject. Sensitivity is usually represented by the symbol d' ('d prime'). When the subject makes mistakes, these tend to veer towards one of two kinds. Either s/he is over-cautious, and makes too many false negatives (i.e. anything s/he is unsure of, s/he rejects), or s/he is over-permissive, and makes too many false positives (i.e. s/he accepts very weak stimuli as signals, even though they could well be noise). The degree of conservatism/liberalism shown by the subject is known as the **response criterion**, often identified by the symbol β (**beta**). The terms 'signal' and 'noise' can refer to realistic external stimuli, and not surprisingly, the analysis has been used extensively in perception. However, the terms can also refer to signals and noise within the neural pathways (e.g. in recalling faint memories from amongst competing 'half-memories'). In its most often-used form, the analysis assumes that the probabilities of a signal being a stimulus or noise can be plotted as separate normal distributions, which partly overlap (the distance between the peaks of the two distributions is d'). Other formats of the analysis are available for dealing with different distributions, and more specialized data sets.

signal detection task Task in which a subject must respond whenever a *target* stimulus occurs.

signal detection theory (SDT) *signal detection analysis.*

signal to noise ratio (SNR) The relative strength of a signal compared to the background *noise* accompanying it. See *signal detection theory.*

silent speech *inner speech.*

Simonides of Ceos An early exponent of the *method of loci technique.* Simonides, an Ancient Greek poet, was a guest at a banquet. For reasons too lengthy to explain here, the banqueting room collapsed just after Simonides had been called outside. The guests were too squashed to be accurately identified, but Simonides was able to identify which body was which by remembering the *mental image* of the seating arrangements.

simple organization (-isation) The term has a variety of meanings, but in discussions of concepts, it can refer to how different items can belong to the same group.

simple reaction time (SRT) See *reaction time.*

simultaneous scanning See *successive scanning.*

single channel theory of attention In its strongest form, the theory that in *selectively attending* to a piece of information, all other pieces of information are totally excluded. In contrast, the *two stage selection model* argues that one piece of information is processed in full,

but other pieces are processed in less depth.

SIS *sensory information store.*

situational memory (SM) Memory for a general situation. This is a more general memory than *event memory*, which is for specific events or types of events.

SIU *Semantic Information Unit.*

size effect (visual imagery) The phenomenon whereby, in scanning a mental image, it takes longer to 'see' details of it when the subject has been told to make the whole image small than when s/he has been told to make the image big.

slave system Sub-system in a larger model which is fully reliant on a *central processor* for provision of information to process, and perhaps for the allocation of its working parameters.

sleep teaching Learning method in which the subject is played auditory material whilst asleep. The amount of information learnt varies according to which stage of sleep the information is played in, but generally, results are not very encouraging for those students looking for an effortless revision method.

slip of the tongue An unintentional speech error. Some (e.g. the *morpheme exchange error, Spoonerism*, etc.) can indicate the nature of the psychological processes governing speech production.

slips of action Mistakes resulting from making inappropriate actions. See *associative activation, capture error, confusions/blends, data-driven error, false triggering, goal switches, programme assembly failures, repetition errors, Spoonerism*, and *unintentional activation.* See also *storage failures* and *test failures.*

slots (schema theory) *attributes.*

SM *situational memory.*

small level units *low level process.*

SNR *signal to noise ratio.*

SOA *stimulus onset asynchrony.*

social cognition The intellectual processes involved in understanding social situations.

software See *hardware.*

source amnesia See *amnesia.*

source node See *spreading activation.*

source problem See *problem isomorphs.*

spacing effect A phenomenon derived from the following experimental design. Subjects are presented with a list of items, one at a time, to remember. The items are presented more than once. The longer the *lag* between presentations, the greater the chance that the item will be subsequently remembered.

span Abbreviation of *memory span* – simply, the number of items a person can remember. Strongly correlated with intelligence (particularly *fluid intelligence*). *Short-term span* is a measure of how many items can be remembered where recall is immediately or very shortly after the list of to-be-remembered items has been presented. This can be assessed in several ways (e.g. the longest length which the subject can accurately recall on 50% of occasions). *Long-term span* is a measure of how many items can be remembered from a set presented some time ago (typically, at least thirty minutes, and often longer). Span can also be classified according to the nature of the to-be-remembered items. Hence, *verbal span* = words; *digit span* = numbers, etc. *Span of apprehension* is the span for visual items which have been presented for a very brief period of time.

span of apprehension See *span.*

spatial See *visuo-spatial.*

spatial ability The ability to judge and manipulate spatial information (i.e. the relative position of items in a space).

spatial inference *Inference* of the position of one location relative to another.

spatial invariance The phenomenon whereby components of some items remain in the same position relative to each other, although their overall appearance may alter (e.g. faces look different, but eyes, noses, lips, etc., are in the same positions relative to each other). See *visuo-spatial.*

spatial metaphor A representation of the structure of the mind in which different mental functions and stores are conceived in terms of items in a space (e.g. like boxes placed in different parts of a room). The metaphor is useful in conveying basic information, but should not be taken as an accurate representation of the physical structure of the brain.

special factor A specialized intellectual skill, hypothesized to operate on its own or in tandem with *g*.

special mechanism model (speech perception) *motor theory of speech perception.*

specific equivalence See *functional equivalence.*

specific memory Memory of a particular event. Compare with *generic memory.*

specific model of working memory (WMS) See *working memory.*

'specious present' William James's description of *short-term memory.*

speech act A verbal utterance designed to convey a statement of emotional state, or of intent to act or to have the listener react. See *commissive, declarative, directive* and *expressive.*

speech code See *articulatory representation.*

speech output lexicon *Mental lexicon* which stores memories of how to produce speech sounds.

speed-accuracy tradeoff (1) On any task in which both speed and accuracy of response are important (e.g. a *fluid intelligence* test, or a *choice reaction time* task), the degree to which the subject is prepared to go faster and risk making more errors. (2) *response-signal technique*.

speed-error tradeoff function *speed-accuracy tradeoff.*

speed test See *power test*.

spelling consistency *consistency (spelling)*.

spelling regularity *regular spelling*.

spelling-to-sound regularity See *regular spelling*.

Sperling's partial report procedure *Partial report procedure* devised by Sperling. Subjects are presented with three rows of letters/digits for a very brief time period using a *tachistoscope*. Immediately or very soon after the stimulus has disappeared, the subjects are played a *probe* of a musical tone – a high tone indicates that they should say what they saw on the top row; a middle tone, the middle row; and a low tone, the bottom row. Provided they are given the tone under a second after the display has disappeared, the subjects are reasonably accurate at recall. This is taken as proof of *iconic memory*.

spillover effect The effect that processing an item has on processing subsequent items.

split brain patient Patient who has had the connections between the left and right *hemispheres* severed (for a medical reason, such as to prevent certain kinds of very serious epileptic fits). The patients often complain that they simulta-neously experience two different worlds.

split span procedure See *dichotic listening task*.

spontaneous generalization (-isation) Term used in *parallel distributed processing* to denote the retrieval of *implicit memories*.

spontaneous pop-up *pop-up*.

Spoonerism (1) Error of speech in which the initial letters of two words in the same phrase are exchanged. Named after the Reverend Spooner (1844–1930), apocryphally famous for such verbal gaffes as (on dismissing a student — Spooner was an Oxford don) 'you have deliberately tasted two worms and you can leave Oxford by the town drain'. Not to be confused with a *morpheme exchange error*. (2) A *slip of action* in which the subject reverses the appropriate sequence of actions.

spread of activation *spreading activation*.

spreading activation The *excitation* of a neuron or unit in a *network*, which causes the excitation of connected neurons/units. This is a concept used in many *propositional network* and *semantic network* models. When a node is stimulated, it in turn stimulates other nodes with which it is connected. This stimulation can be sufficient to fire them into life, or can place them in a state of readiness, so that less excitation is required subsequently to activate them into life (this can account for e.g. *semantic facilitation*). Nodes are assumed to be connected to each other with different strengths, chiefly dependent upon the degree to which they have been associated in the past. E.g. nodes representing 'sheep' and 'cow' will be more strongly connected than nodes for 'sheep' and 'Botany Bay'. The stronger the link, the more excitation one node will receive from the other. However, the more links a node has with other nodes, the slower the rate at which the other nodes are activated (the *fan effect*). The first node to be stimulated is called the *source node*.

spreading activation model *Network model* originally devised by Collins and Quillian, and using the principles of *spreading activation*.

spurious activation See *target activation*.

SQ3R method Method of studying a lengthy piece of prose (e.g. a textbook chapter), similar in format to the *PQ4R method*.

SRT (1) *simple reaction time*. (2) *serial reaction time*.

SSRT *serial simple reaction time*.

stages (of processing) *processing stages*.

Stanford–Binet Scale/Test *IQ* test – the first to be standardized. Based on original work by Binet, standardized by Terman at Stanford University. Revised several times, and still in common use.

start state (problem solving) *initial state (problem solving)*.

STAS *short-term auditory store*.

state action tree A diagrammatic representation of the choices available at progressive stages of an act (typically problem-solving). The choices are represented as 'branches' spreading out from a *node*. Each branch terminates in another node. Each of these nodes in turn has branches emanating from it, indicating the choices available if it is selected, etc.

state-dependency See *context-dependency*.

state-dependent learning (1) *state-dependency*. (2) Less accurately, *encoding specificity*.

stem completion task *Completion task* in which the subject must complete a word when given a section of it.

Stent-Singer rule Type of *Hebbian rule*. If a receiving unit is active, and a unit capable of sending a signal to it is also active (i.e. it is sending a signal) then the *weight* of the connection is strengthened. However, if a unit capable of sending a signal is inactive, then the weight is decreased. Nothing occurs if the receiving unit is inactive.

step tracking See *tracking*.

stereotype A *schema* or overgeneralized image – usually with the implication that the portrayal is over-simplistic and/or unfavourable.

Sternberg test A *recognition* test in which the subject is shown a small group of items, and must then indicate whether a presented item belongs to the set just seen.

stimulus-driven processing *bottom-up processing*.

stimulus ensemble The total set of items which may be used in an experiment.

stimulus onset asynchrony (SOA) (1) The interval between the onset of one stimulus (e.g. a *warning signal*) and the onset of the next (e.g. the *target*). (2) In a *masking* experiment, the difference between the length of time the item has to be presented alone, and the length of time it has to be presented when it is followed by a *mask*, in order for it to be correctly recognized.

stimulus-response (S-R) learning (1) Type of learning associated with *behaviourism* – the stimulus given to the subject and the response made to the stimulus are measured, but (in rigid versions of the theory) no assumption is made about the subject's thought processes in making the response. (2) More generally, learning the appropriate response to a stimulus.

stimulus suffix effect In a test of *recall*, the effect of presenting an item at or towards the end of a list which is not to be recalled. This mars recall of the final few items on the list.

STM *short-term memory.*

stochastic sequence A sequence of events, each of which can assume several forms, and where the probability of one form being chosen is solely or partly dependent on the nature of the previous events.

stop consonant (phonetics) *plosive (phonetics).*

storage capacity *memory capacity.*

storage failures *repetition errors.*

storage models of memory Generic name for a variety of models of memory which concentrate on the structure of the memory stores, rather than on how the information is placed in the stores. Some commentators have criticized this approach – e.g. see *levels of processing.*

storage processes See *information processing.*

story grammar The degree to which a story follows the conventions of plot and narrative. Writing which is ungrammatical in this sense is extremely difficult to understand (e.g. James Joyce's 'Finnigan's Wake'). See *story schema.*

story recall The process of recalling a story or other large piece of prose/poetry. For most people, this entails recalling the plot and occasional details, rather than verbatim reproduction.

story schema Knowledge of conventions of plot and narrative (probable reason why television drama becomes increasingly tedious the older one gets). Compare with *event schema,* and see *story grammar.*

strategic A term used in a rather nebulous manner, but generally, pertaining to any mental process in which there is conscious planning.

strategic learning Learning the optimal manner in which to solve problems of a particular type.

strength (memory) The difficulty with which a memory is lost/supplanted by other items. The harder it is to lose/supplant, the stronger it is said to be.

strengthening In the *ACT* model, the phenomenon whereby the more often a *production* is used, the faster it can be operated.

strong AI The belief that an *artificial intelligence* programme could potentially represent the working of the mind, to the extent that the computer could be said to have a mind of its own. This contrasts with **weak AI**, which argues that although the programme and mind might have complete *functional equivalence,* the computer could not be said to have a mind. See *Chinese Room.*

strong equivalence (artificial intelligence/computer simulation) See *functional equivalence.*

Stroop test Experimental technique named after its creator. Subjects are shown the names of colours, printed in coloured ink. The colour name and the ink colour may match (e.g. the word 'green' printed in green ink), or they may not (e.g. the word 'purple' printed in red ink). The subject's task is to name the colour of the ink. Most subjects find the task very difficult when the ink colour and name do not match.

structuralism Guiding principle of Wilhelm Wundt and many other early psychologists that mental processes could, by *introspection*, be broken down into a set of basic, simple structures. Although such an extreme view has long since been rejected, the term is still loosely used to denote the analysis of components of mental acts.

structures, mental *mental structures.*

STS *short-term store.*

STSS *short-term sensory store.*

STVS *short-term visual store.*

sub-cortical Pertaining to areas of the brain other than the *cerebral cortex.*

sub-goal The intended aim of a component stage of an activity (e.g. in driving to work, there might be a 'getting into the car' sub-goal, 'reversing down the drive' sub-goal, etc.). The term is used to describe a component stage a subject must accomplish in a problem-solving task.

sub-goal decomposition Examining an activity in terms of its *sub-goals.* The term is used of planning the stages of activity in problem-solving tasks.

sub-morphemic Pertaining to items which are at a 'lower' level than the *morpheme* (e.g. *graphemes*, letter features, etc.).

subitization (-isation) *subitizing.*

subitizing The instant realization of how many items there are in a display without having to count them one-by-one.

subject (experimental design) Participant in an experiment.

subject (linguistics) In a phrase, the subject is the agent performing the action described (e.g. 'the BOY kicked the ball'). The *object* of the sentence is who or what the action is directed towards (e.g. 'the boy kicked the BALL').

subjective threshold See *threshold.*

subjective utility A subject's personal estimate of the usefulness of an item or event.

sublexical Pertaining to any process which occurs before the *lexicon* is accessed.

subliminal Pertaining to a stimulus too weak to be consciously detected. However, subsequent behaviour may indicate that it was detected 'unconsciously' (e.g. an item presented subliminally may subsequently be selected from a set of items at a higher-than-chance level). By extension of this principal, *subliminal learning* is the acquisition and possession of knowledge which one is unaware of having been explicitly taught.

subliminal learning See *subliminal.*

subordinate category Category which encompasses fewer or no other categories and is more specific in its contents than a *superordinate category*. E.g. the category of 'cats' is subordinate to the superordinate category of 'mammals'.

subordinate level (1) A lower level. (2) *subordinate category.*

subroutine failure Type of *slip of action* in which the subject makes any type of error in the ordering of a sequence of actions.

substitution error In reading, perception, memory, etc., replacing the *target item* with another item (often related).

substitution priming See *priming.*

subtraction method Method of assessing the speed of a particular mental process. The subject is given two tasks, identical except that one contains an extra mental task. The difference in time required to do the two tasks is taken as a measure of how long the extra mental task takes to perform. The approach has a specious charm, but is open to criticism. See *chronometric analysis*.

subtraction solution See *water jar problem*.

subtractive bilingualism See *additive bilingualism*.

subvocal rehearsal Rehearsing to-be-remembered material using *subvocal speech*.

subvocal speech (1) *inner speech*. (2) Minute movements of the muscles involved in speech exhibited when a subject is thinking/reading.

subvocalization (-isation) *subvocal speech*.

successive scanning In problem-solving and *concept formation*, considering one hypothesis at a time. This contrasts with *simultaneous scanning*, in which the subject begins with a set of hypotheses, and gradually eliminates these as more evidence is collected.

suffix effect Typically, an abbreviation of the *auditory suffix effect*, but the *stimulus suffix effect* may instead be indicated.

superordinate category See *subordinate category*.

superordinate level (1) A higher level. (2) *superordinate category*.

supervisory activating system (SAS) See *SAS model*.

supervisory attentional system Hypothesized mechanism responsible for *controlled processing*.

suppression The conscious submerging of unpleasant ideas and memories. Contrast with *repression*.

supraspan learning Learning lists of items whose length exceeds one's *memory span*.

surface *shallow*.

surface dysgraphia A complex failure of writing – patients have most problems with *low frequency* words, which may be partially correctly spelt; or similar-sounding words may be erroneously offered; or may be spelt as *psendohomophones*, but with the required pronunciation (e.g. 'kee' for 'quay').

surface dyslexia An *acquired dyslexia* – the patient shows a complex set of symptoms, which most closely resemble a child learning to read. Some words are immediately correctly read, but others have to be 'sounded out', or are pronounced as a word which looks like the to-be-read word.

surface representation *surface*.

surface structure See *Chomsky's theory of language*.

sustained attention The ability to concentrate on a set task without being distracted.

syllabary *syllabic writing system*.

syllabic writing system Writing system in which symbols represent the *syllables* of the language.

syllable The smallest unit of a word whose pronunciation forms a rhythmic break when spoken (e.g. 'transubstantiation' is a six-syllable word, 'yes' is a one-syllable word). A syllable can be subdivided into its **onset** (the initial sound) and its **rime** (the remaining sounds).

syllable boundary The point in a word at which one *syllable* ends and another begins.

syllogism A statement consisting of three premises, of which the third is a conclusion drawn from the first two (e.g. 'all As are B; all Bs are C; therefore, all As are C').

symbolic distance effect *distance effect (visual imagery)*.

symbolic fallacy Term used in several variants, but essentially refers to the failure of (cognitive) psychologists to relate their neat models and symbolism to real life psychological performance.

symmetry heuristic Phenomenon whereby subjects tend to use the *heuristic* that items are more regularly planned than they really are, thereby making processing/remembering easier but less accurate.

synergic See *synergism.*

synergism The joint action of several factors aiming at a common goal. There is often the implication that the joint action is greater than the sum of the individual components. The adjective derived from synergism is *synergic.*

synergistic ecphory The process of retrieving a memory by combining the *retrieval cue* with the memory trace.

synergy *synergism.*

synonym-antonym test Test in which the subject must decide if word pairs mean the same or are opposites.

synonym test Test in which the subject must supply a word meaning the same as one supplied by the experimenter.

syntactic Pertaining to *syntax.*

syntactic rules The set of grammatical dictums which determine what is correct or incorrect grammar in the language in question.

syntactic sentence Sentence which is grammatically correct; however, the term usually carries the implication that it has a nonsensical meaning (e.g. 'the transparent turquoise penguin ratified the thoughtful banana').

syntactic theory *abstract rule theory.*

syntactic tree *Tree structure diagram* demonstrating the *syntactic* structure of a sentence.

syntactic violation Phrase or sentence which, although conveying a sensible meaning, is ungrammatical (e.g. 'she done him wrong'). This contrasts with a *semantic violation*, in which the phrase or sentence is grammatically correct, but otherwise meaningless (e.g. Chomsky's example – 'colourless green ideas sleep furiously').

syntax grammar.

synthetic statement A statement whose truth or falsehood can only be determined by reference to the outside world.

systemic awareness Knowledge of how one's memory works (including how to make memorization easier, how easy different items are to remember, etc.). Compare with *epistemic awareness.* See also *feeling of knowing, metamemory* and *metaknowledge.*

systematic random search Systematically searching for the correct answer through the total list of possibilities, without any guiding strategy for narrowing the list of items to be searched through.

T

T-scope *tachistoscope.*

tachistoscope (T-scope) An instrument for presenting visual stimuli for very brief periods of time (*tachistoscopic presentation*).

tachistoscopic presentation See *tachistoscope.*

tactical learning Learning that a particular problem-solving stage used in one task can be applied to similar tasks, thereby improving problem-solving speed.

target *target item.*

target activation In a *mental model* (particularly one in *parallel distributed processing*), the production of the correct response. A *spurious activation* is the production of an inappropriate response.

target item The correct answer to the task in question. The term is frequently used in the *visual search* paradigm, but also describes e.g. the previously-encountered word embedded in a *recognition* experiment. See *distractor item.*

target problem See *problem isomorphs.*

task environment In problem-solving tasks, the problem and the available materials and options as presented by the experiment. Using this terminology, the *problem space* may be viewed specifically as the range perceived by the subject.

TAU *thematic abstraction unit.*

T.B. Pseudonym of the *amnesic* patient in an often cited case study, with an especially impaired *short-term memory.*

TBF *to-be-forgotten.*

TBR *to-be-remembered.*

Teachable Language Comprehender (TLC) A *network model* dealing with the categorization of items. The model was a forerunner of the *spreading activation model.*

technical knowledge See *natural knowledge.*

template matching Name given to a variety of theories of pattern recognition. At its simplest, the theory argues that the mind recognizes a pattern (e.g. a letter) by matching it against a mental image (template) of the pattern. However, the theory in its simplest form is untenable, since it assumes that we possess a different template for every pattern we recognize (e.g. we must have templates for letters in every printing type and handwriting style). This is impossible, since we can recognize millions of different patterns, and we could not store unique templates for all of them. Although much maligned in its simplest form, the template theory gave rise to more sophisticated models of pattern recognition.

template theory *template matching.*

temporal inference *Inference* of when an event occurred. See *forward telescoping.*

temporal lobes Section of the *cerebral cortex* occupying, roughly speaking, the area of the left and right temples. Their chief function is interpreting information – in most individuals the left temporal lobe is essential in comprehending and producing speech and writing.

They are also strongly involved in the storage of memories.

temporal order judgement (TOJ) A judgement from memory of the order in which a set of items was presented.

TEP *transitional error probability.*

terminal node In a *tree structure diagram*, or other representations of a process using *nodes*, the node representing the output of the process described.

tertiary auditory cortex See *primary auditory cortex.*

tertiary cortex See *primary cortex.*

test failures *goal switches.*

test smart subjects *test wise subjects.*

test statistics Any method of assessing the statistical properties of tests.

test wise subjects Subjects who have been given so many psychology tests that they score higher marks than would be predicted on any further tests, because they are used to the general procedures and wiles of psychologists and their testing procedures (the *carryover effect*).

text model A mental representation of a piece of text.

texture gradient See *Gibson's theory of direct perception.*

TFF *two flash fusion.*

the propositional calculus *Propositional calculus* – it is traditional (but by no means obligatory) to use the 'the' prefix.

thematic abstraction unit (TAU) A mechanism for abstracting the theme of an argument or situation. See *thematic organization packet.*

thematic organization (-isation) packet (TOP) A mechanism for abstracting conceptual links between different situations (e.g. being jilted by a girlfriend or boyfriend and losing a business con-

tract). TOPs are usually presented as a higher level version of *memory organization packets (MOPs).*

theory of identical elements See *doctrine of formal discipline.*

THOG task Measure of reasoning in which the subject is presented with a variety of shapes, which differ in two ways – outline and colour. In the basic version of the task, the subject is told that a shape is classified as a 'THOG' if it has either a particular colour or a particular outline, but it is not a THOG if it possesses both simultaneously or neither (e.g. if the colour and outline in question are red and triangle, then a red square is a THOG, a blue triangle is a THOG, but a red triangle or a white square are not THOGs). There are several variants of the basic task.

thought experiment *gedanken experiment.*

thought suppression (1) *suppression.* (2) more generally, attempting to suppress a particular thought (such as trying not to think about something stated by the experimenter – see *white bear experiment*).

three coins problem Test of problem-solving ability. The subject is presented with three coins on a table, two showing tails, and one heads. On each move, two coins must be turned over simultaneously. In precisely three such moves, how can the coins all show heads or all show tails?

3-D model representation See *Marr's computational theory.*

three store memory model Model of memory which assumes three principal *mnemonic* mechanisms (namely, *sensory memory, short-term memory* and *long-term memory*). See e.g. the *modal memory model.*

three-term series problem *syllogism.*

threshold The intensity of stimulation required to notice a difference in the stimulus. An *absolute threshold* is the lowest level of stimulation at which the stimulus can be detected (e.g. the dimmest light which can be seen). See *catch trials*. The *difference threshold* is the smallest difference between two stimuli which can be reliably (not necessarily always) noticed (e.g. how much brighter one light has to be than another for the difference to be detected). The *interval of uncertainty* is the difference between the minimum intensity necessary always to notice a change, and the maximum intensity where the change is never noticed. In between these intensities, there is a probability that the difference will be detected – this probability increases the stronger the intensity. The difference threshold is calculated as the intensity where the difference is noticed on x% of occasions (the value of x varies between commentators – 50% and 75% are popular choices). The smallest change necessary to evoke a perception of change is known as the *just noticeable difference*, and the largest change which does not evoke a perception of change is known as the *just not noticeable difference*. See *Weber's law*. To take account of *subliminal* perception, thresholds can also be categorized as *objective thresholds* (the threshold at which nothing is perceived, either consciously or unconsciously) and *subjective thresholds* (the threshold at which the subject may be consciously unaware of the stimulus, although there is evidence of subliminal perception).

threshold hypothesis An (unproven) argument that items in *long-term memory* are stored at a particular 'strength'. Over time this strength declines (unless the

item is rehearsed), until it drops below a *threshold*, whereupon it can no longer be retrieved. It is assumed that the threshold for *recognition* is lower than that for *recall* (hence why some items cannot be voluntarily brought to mind, but can nonetheless be recognized).

time on target (TOT) In an experiment where the subject must track an object, the number of times that s/he is successful in doing this.

time-sharing (1) *postponement model*. (2) The alternation between performing two or more tasks.

time sharing tasks *concurrent tasks*.

tip of the tongue (TOT) Phenomenon whereby an item cannot be fully recovered from memory, but a lot of its features (e.g. number of syllables, words which sound like it, etc.) can be identified: i.e. the word is on the 'tip of the tongue'. The phenomenon illustrates how memories may be stored or retrieved piecemeal rather than as whole chunks which are recovered in an 'all or nothing' fashion. A popular method of generating TOT states was created by Brown and McNeill, who provided subjects with definitions of obscure words, and asked the subjects to provide the word being described.

TLC *Teachable Language Comprehender*.

to-be-forgotten (TBF) See *directed forgetting*.

to-be-remembered (TBR) Pertaining to items in a memory task which the subject must remember.

TOJ *temporal order judgement*.

token (semantic memory) Memory of a specific example of a category. This is contrasted with a *type*, which is a memory of a category.

token distractor See *distractor item*.

TOP *thematic organization packet.*

top-down processing Identifying an object by 'guessing' what it might be, and then seeking evidence to prove the hypothesis. Often the 'guess' is based on partial information gleaned from *bottom-up processing*. E.g. suppose that a subject has already identified the first two letters of 'CAT'. The top-down process might assume that in order to make a real word, the next letter will have to be B,D,M,N,P,R,T, or W. Hence, it might direct the bottom-up process to search for features of those letters, and not to be so vigorous in searching for components of 'unsuitable' letters.

top layer (parallel distributed processing) See *layer (parallel distributed processing).*

TOT (1) *tip of the tongue.* (2) *time on target.*

total perceptual span See *perceptual span.*

total time hypothesis (learning) The phenomenon whereby, in general, the longer one spends practising a skill, the better it gets.

Tower of Hanoi problem Problem-solving task comprising three rings of progressively smaller size and three vertical pegs arrayed in a straight line. At the start of the task, the rings are placed on one of the outermost pegs, with the rings in order of size, the smallest at the top. The subject's task is to move the rings to the other outermost peg. The rings can only be moved one at a time, on to any of the pegs, with the proviso that a larger ring never is placed over a smaller one.

TRACE *Artificial intelligence* speech perception model.

trace decay theory of forgetting The theory that *memory traces* automatically become weaker over time if they are not rehearsed. This contrasts with the *interference theory of forgetting*, which argues that memories are lost because they are supplanted by newer memories, which interfere with them.

tracking Any task in which a moving display must be followed (with the eyes, or more commonly, by moving a finger or pointer). There are three basic types of task. In *pursuit tracking*, an item must be tracked around a course or track. *Compensatory tracking* requires the subject to keep a moving item (which, given free rein, would move continuously) in one position, or as near to that position as possible. *Step tracking* is a refinement of this, in which the item moves in fits and starts.

trade-off The degree to which maximum efficiency in one process must be offset in order to allow for an acceptable level of performance in another process. A well-known example of this is the *speed-accuracy tradeoff.*

transcortical aphasia An *aphasia* combining symptoms of both *transcortical motor aphasia* and *transcortical sensory aphasia.*

transcortical motor aphasia *Aphasia* in which there is no spontaneous production of language, although the patient can accurately repeat what has been just been said by someone else.

transcortical sensory aphasia *Aphasia* in which there is no comprehension of language, although the patient can repeat what is said to him/her, and speech is conventionally enunciated (although its meaning is usually unintelligible).

transfer appropriate processing Processing information (particularly memorizing items) in a manner best suited for future use. E.g. in memorizing a sequence of historical events, the wording used will be of secondary importance to the conveyance of dates, etc. Conversely, in memorizing a poem, it is the exact wording which needs to be remembered above the need to convey meaning or argument.

transfer of skill The degree to which an acquired skill can aid performance of other skills (e.g. does enhancing performance at *digit span* improve memory for pictures?). See *doctrine of formal discipline*.

transformational grammar See *Chomsky's theory of language*.

transition network Model for processing the *syntactic* content of statements. The model processes the sentence and, upon recognizing the syntactic nature of a word, creates an anticipation of what the next word's category should be if the sentence is to be grammatical. There are a number of permutations of the model. See *augmented transition network* and *recursive augmented transition network*.

transitional error probability (TEP) In recalling a sentence, the probability of incorrectly recalling the next word if the previous word has been correctly recalled.

transparent See *opaque*.

transparent system See *opaque system*.

transposition task Test of problem-solving ability/logical reasoning, in which the knowledge of how to solve a problem must be applied to a similar but not identical task.

travelling salesman problem A test of planning. Subjects play the roles of sales personnel who have to travel to and visit a number of shops in a single working day, planning their routes, the order of visits, etc.

tree structure diagram Diagrammatic representation of the structure of a process into layers of increasing detail. Often used to show how a sentence can be broken down into units of *noun phrases* and *verb phrases*, and from this to increasing levels of detail (e.g. in *phrase-structure grammar*).

tricode theory Any theory which proposes that mental processes can be encoded in three separate but related ways (e.g. verbal, *visuo-spatial* and abstract).

trigram Group of three letters which may from a real word, but usually do not. A *consonant trigram* is a group of three consonants. A *CVC trigram* is a group consisting of a consonant-vowel-consonant (e.g., 'buf', 'wek', etc.).

true negative See *true positive*.

true positive Correctly identifying a signal or *target* as a signal or target, rather than rejecting it as an extraneous piece of information. Similarly, a *true negative* is the correct rejection of background noise or other extraneous information, because it is not a signal or target. The inaccurate rejection of a signal/target is a *false negative*, whilst the incorrect acceptance of an extraneous piece of information/noise as a signal/target is a *false positive*. See *signal detection analysis*.

true score See *true scores theory*.

true scores theory The argument that a subject's test score is composed of his/her *true score* (reflecting his/her real worth), plus or minus a margin of error (the *absolute error*).

truth table A diagrammatic representation of a *proposition*, used in some versions of formal logic.

tuning (1) Adding relatively minor information to a *schema* (i.e. which does not alter its basic structure). Compare with *accretion* and *restructuring*. (2) In skill acquisition, making the excution of the skill faster and more appropriate to the situation.

2AFC See *recognition task*.

2.5-D sketch See *Marr's computational theory*.

two concept theory of memory A theory of memory which classifies memories according to their degree of *activation* and their *strength*.

two factor theory of memory A theory of memory which classifies memories into *episodic memory* and *semantic memory*.

two flash fusion (TFF) Measure of the minimum time gap between two flashes necessary for the subject to (mis)perceive them as a single flash. See *critical flicker fusion*.

two phase motor unit Phenomenon whereby in making a movement towards a target, the initial movement is very rapid, but not over-accurate, and is followed by a more accurate and guided movement which is slower. The phenomenon is only seen in movements which are overall relatively slow.

two process theory of memory A theory of memory which classifies the process of memory into *recall* and *recognition*. Recall is regarded as requiring the process of retrieving the information and the process of judging whether it is correct, whilst recognition requires only the latter.

two stage selection model See *single channel theory of attention*.

two string problem See *functional fixedness*.

type (semantic memory) See *token (semantic memory)*.

type change distractor See *distractor item*.

type I processing See *levels of processing*.

type II processing See *levels of processing*.

typeface *font*.

typicality A measure of how representative an item is of a particular category (e.g. 'carrot' is a very typical member of the vegetable family, whilst 'asparagus' is not).

typicality gradient A representation of the *typicality* of different items belonging to the same category.

U

ugly sister effect A phenomenon whereby in a *tip of the tongue* state, subjects often produce an erroneous word, which *blocks* access to the sought-for word, and which cannot be expunged.

ultimate constituent See *constituent (psycholinguistics)*.

unattended information In an *attention* task, information which is not consciously attended to (but which may nonetheless be processed – see e.g. the *cocktail party phenomenon*).

unattended message The information which is not attended to in a *selective attention* task.

unattended priming The phenomenon that under certain circumstances, stimuli, although not consciously attended to, can *prime* a subject.

unattended speech effect The phenomenon whereby speech, although unattended to, can still disrupt memory for verbal materials. The speech need not necessarily be in a language the subject understands.

unattended stimulus A stimulus which is present, but to which the subject is told not to attend during the course of an experiment.

UNDERSTAND A computerized problem-solving programme (e.g. used on the *monster problem*).

unintentional activation A *slip of action* in which an inappropriate action (which is part of another sequence) is performed during a sequence of appropriate actions.

unitary process The theory or assumption that two or more processes share the same mechanisms, or operate in a qualitatively and/or quantitatively similar manner.

unitary psychology The belief that the traditional divisions/specialisms in psychology (cognition, developmental psychology, individual differences, etc.) create artificial barriers and that the mind can only be realistically treated as a cohesive whole. Compare with *modular psychology*.

universal quantifier Term used in formal logic. Corresponds most closely to the word 'all'.

unlearning Forgetting a list of items and/or deliberately replacing one memorized list with another.

unrelated items See *related items*.

unvoiced (phonetics) See *voiced (phonetics)*.

upper case See *case*.

V

values See *attributes.*

vanishing cues method See *method of vanishing cues.*

variables (schema theory) *attributes.*

varied mapping (VM) See *consistent mapping.*

varied set procedure See *positive set.*

verb phrase (VP) A portion of a sentence which contains a verb (and where applicable, adverbs, etc.) indicating what the *subject* of the sentence did. See *noun phrase (NP).*

verbal code Storage of information which is subjectively perceived as a set of words or a voice in the head.

verbal fluency measure Any measure which assesses the ease with which a subject can produce verbal information. A typical test might be to see how many words beginning with a particular letter can be produced within a time limit, or how many words can be formed out of the letters in another word (a type of *word fluency test*).

verbal mediation See *mediation.*

verbal protocol A subject's spoken commentary on his or her performance on a task (usually while actually performing the task) and/or on his/her thought processes (i.e. thinking aloud).

verbal skills Any skill or collection of skills with a heavy or sole emphasis on verbal materials.

verbal span See *span.*

verbatim memory A memory which exactly reproduces the to-be-remembered material. For substantially-sized pieces of information, usually only found for items which have been learnt by rote (e.g. pieces of poetry learnt at school). See *reproductive memory.*

veridical The true representation.

verification reaction time (VRT) *verification time.*

verification time *Reaction time* to give a 'true/false type answer.

vigilance The ability to sustain attention or alertness over a (usually lengthy) period of time.

violation error See *preservation error.*

visual See *visuo-spatial.*

visual cortex *Occipital lobe* – area of cortex responsible for visual perception.

visual duration threshold The minimum length of time a stimulus must be displayed for it to be reliably identified.

visual error (reading) *visual reading error.*

visual masking See *masking.*

visual modality Pertaining to any stimuli which can be seen.

visual reading Recognizing words by their shape, and without the use of *phonic mediation.* Invaluable strategy in reading *irregular spellings* (e.g. 'quay' can only be correctly pronounced using visual reading). For obvious reasons, visual reading can only be used on words already encountered, and accordingly, cannot be used to read new or *nonsense words.*

visual reading error Misreading a word for one which looks similar (e.g. 'cabbage' for 'cribbage').

visual representation A *mental image* stored in what is subjectively perceived as a visual image.

visual search Term for any experimental paradigm in which the subject must visually search an array of items for an item. The item being searched for is called the *target item*, and the other items present are called the *distractor items*. By varying the level of similarity between the target and the distractors, the time taken to complete the task will vary. It is assumed that the longer it takes the subject, the harder s/he finds it to distinguish between target and distractor. This information is of use e.g. in determining what are salient features in pattern recognition.

visual segmentation error *migration error*.

visual-then-semantic error Making a *visual reading error* followed by a *semantic error*. E.g. misreading 'car', as 'hearts', (car → card → hearts).

visual type See *auditory type*.

visual word form system *visual word recognition system*.

visual word recognition system Hypothesized reading process responsible for recognizing the shape of the whole word.

visuo-spatial Pertaining to anything which is *visual* (what something looks like) and/or *spatial* (where items are located in space, or relative to each other).

visuo-spatial scratchpad *visuo-spatial sketchpad*.

visuo-spatial sketchpad See *working memory*.

VM *varied mapping*.

voice key Electronic switch activated by the voice. Can be used e.g. in *reaction time* experiments when conventional button-pressing is for some reason inappropriate.

voiced (phonetics) Pertaining to a *phone* whose production involves an exhalation of air from the lungs (e.g. vowels). In contrast, an **unvoiced** phone does not involve air exhaled from the lungs (e.g. the first sound in 'kick).

voluntary memory A memory which has been deliberately recalled by the subject. Contrast with *involuntary memory*.

Von Restorff effect The phenomenon whereby an item which appears different from other items in a list is remembered more effectively.

VP (1) *verb phrase*. (2) Pseudonym of an exceptionally gifted *mnemonist*.

VRT *verification reaction time*.

W

WAIS *Wechsler Adult Intelligence Scale.*

War of the Ghosts An American Indian folk tale, used in an ingenious experiment by Bartlett to demonstrate *schema theory.* The subjects were native English, and were presented with the story to read. The War of the Ghosts has a narrative style and imagery which are unknown in Western literature, and which accordingly makes very confusing reading for Westernized subjects. Bartlett's subjects were asked to recall the story at intervals ranging from immediately after reading to several months or years later. As a general rule, the subjects' recollection replaced the 'ethnic' elements of the story with Western stereotypical narrative patterns, and this process was more exaggerated the longer the delay before recall. See *reality monitoring*

warning signal The warning to a subject that a signal requiring a response is about to be presented. See *response signal.*

Washoe Chimpanzee taught to use American sign language. Washoe was able to learn to communicate in a (by human standards) rudimentary fashion. Whether she was using language as a genuinely symbolic communication has been debated. A similar debate surrounds the chimpanzee *Nim*, who was also taught sign language.

Wason card task A test of *conditional reasoning* by Wason and colleagues. Subjects were shown four cards, respectively bearing the symbols, E,K,4 and 7. They were told that if a card had a vowel on one side, then there was an even number on the other. Which cards should be turned over to check this rule? A number of permutations of this task have been used, and generally, if the task is made more realistic, then performance improves.

Wason's selection task *Wason card task.*

Wason's 2-4-6 task Task in which subjects must uncover the rule behind creating triplets of numbers. Subjects are told that '2,4,6' is an example of the rule, and then the subjects produce sets of three numbers which they are told are either correct or wrong.

watchkeeping task A measure of *vigilance* – the subject must observe a display, and indicate when there is any change (which occurs rarely, hence testing vigilance).

water jar problem Test of intelligence/problem-solving ability, in which, given a set of containers of known volumes, the subject must decide how they can measure a specified quantity. E.g. 'there are four jars which can hold 2, 2000, 40 and 20 litres – how can exactly 2 litres be measured?'. An *addition solution* is simply to add the contents of jugs to each other. Similarly, a *subtraction solution* involves subtracting the contents of jugs from each other.

WCST *Wisconsin Card Sorting Task.*

weak AI See *strong AI.*

weak equivalence (artificial intelligence/computer simulation) See *functional equivalence.*

weak knowledge Knowledge which is *domain-general*, and accordingly, although applicable across many situations, may not be specifically useful in any single one of them.

Wearing, Clive *Clive Wearing.*

Weber's law Law which states that the smallest change in intensity which will be noticed, divided by the original intensity of the stimulus, equals a constant. Symbolically represented as $\Delta I / I = K$. It follows from this that the more intense the initial stimulus, the bigger the change needed to evoke a *threshold*. Generally the law holds up for all but extreme intensities of stimulation.

Wechsler Adult Intelligence Scale (WAIS) An adult intelligence test battery covering all commonly assessed areas of intelligence. The tests can be subdivided into those which test verbal skills, and those which have no strong verbal element (the *Performance scales*).

Wechsler-Bellevue Scale Early form of *Wechsler Adult Intelligence Scale.*

weight (1) 'Weighting' refers to any method of adjusting scores to express their relative importance. This can be important e.g. in many statistical and scoring procedures. (2) In *parallel distributed processing*, the (usually adjustable) strength of the connection between two units (e.g. see *Hebbian rules*).

Weinstein maps A set of tests of *visuo-spatial* ability. The subject is presented with nine dots drawn on the floor in a 3 x 3 square pattern. S/he is given a 'map' showing a route to be walked around the dots (the map cannot be turned to keep in the same orientation as the floor pattern). A variety of such routes (of increasing complexity) have to be taken.

well defined problem Problem in which both the *initial state* and *goal state* are clearly defined. See *ill defined problem.*

Wernicke's aphasia *Aphasia* characterized by a failure to comprehend language, although speech may be relatively unimpaired. Contrast with *Broca's aphasia.*

white bear experiment Test of *thought suppression* (definition 2) derived from an anecdote about the Russian novelist Dostoevsky, who mentally tortured a younger brother by repeatedly telling him not to think about a white bear (whereupon the brother could not get the image out of his head). Subjects are asked to try not to think about a white bear for a period of time. Every time the image of a white bear enters their heads, they record the fact.

whole learning See *part learning.*

whole report procedure Memory test in which the subject is requested to report as much of a display/set of stimuli as possible (i.e. rather than being told to concentrate on remembering one aspect of it – see *partial report procedure*). The term is usually reserved for experiments where the stimulus is a visual display presented for a brief period of time using a *tachistoscope.*

wholist strategy Technique employed in a *reception paradigm*. The subject begins by assuming that all features of the item represent the concept. This opinion is adhered to until an item is presented which s/he erroneously rejects or accepts. The concept is then revised so that erroneous features of the old hypothesis are rejected, and new features are accepted. This process is repeated until the correct solution is found. This contrasts with a *partist strategy*, in which the subject only attends to some of the features, and bases his/her hypothesis purely on them. When proved wrong, s/he concentrates on other sets of features.

wholistic processing General term for models of processing which argue that a stimulus is primarily interpreted as a whole unit, rather than in terms of its features.

Whorfian hypothesis *linguistic relativity hypothesis.*

Windrow-Hoff rule *Delta rule.*

width of attention The range of stimuli in a display which can influence a subject's performance on a measure of *attention.*

width of search The limit imposed on the number of options which are explored in e.g. problem solving.

Wisconsin Card Sorting Task (WCST) Measure of hypothesis formation and the ability to reject invalid hypotheses. Accordingly, it is also a measure of perseveration. Subjects must discover the correct rule for matching up cards of differing patterns and colours (e.g. a yellow card must always be matched with a red card, etc.). Once they have discovered the correct rule, the experimenter changes the rule, and how quickly the subject stops using the old rule and searches for the new one is measured, as well as how quickly s/he solves the new problem. The test is used with patients and average subjects. The test was primarily designed to assess patients with brain damage (particularly to the *frontal lobes*).

witness testimony *eyewitness testimony.*

W.L.P. Pseudonym of the patient whose symptoms and behaviour were reported in an often-cited case study of *demented dyslexia.*

WM *working memory.*

WMG *general working memory.*

WMS (1) *working memory span.* (2) *specific model of working memory.*

wolves and sheep problem See *river crossing problem.*

word blend Error (nearly always of speech, rather than writing) in which sections of two words, both of which are appropriate in the place in the sentence, are blended together to form an inappropriate word.

word building test *word fluency test.*

word envelope The overall shape of a word.

word exchange error Error (nearly always of speech, rather than writing) in which words swap places in a statement (e.g. 'the fridge is in the custard').

word fluency test Any *verbal fluency measure* which requires subjects to produce words. Often there are additional requirements – e.g. to produce words beginning with a certain sound, or from a particular category, usually against the clock.

word form dyslexia *letter-by-letter reading.*

word fragment completion (WFC) task *Completion task* in which the subject must complete a word, having been given some of its letters.

word frequency *frequency (words)* .

word frequency effect The phenomenon whereby *high frequency words* are processed more efficiently than *low frequency words.*

word identification span The field of view (the *total perceptual span*) within which word identification is possible.

word length effect The phenomenon whereby fewer long words (i.e. words which take longer to pronounce) can be stored in *short-term memory* than can short words.

word level See *level (mental model)*.

word outline *word shape* (definition 1).

word priming *Priming* in which the *prime* is a word.

word recognition unit Unit in a *mental model* responsible for collecting information from lower level units (e.g. *letter recognition units*). If the information collected is sufficiently similar to the word it represents, then the unit is activated, indicating recognition of that particular word.

word shape (1) The overall contour of the visual shape of a word. (2) More generally, the visual appearance of a word.

word stem completion task *stem completion task*.

word superiority effect (WSE) (1) A counter-intuitive phenomenon whereby a letter can usually be identified faster when it is part of a word than when it is presented in isolation. (2) The phenomenon whereby a real word is better recognized than a *nonsense word*.

working backwards technique Problem-solving method in which the subject breaks the final *goal* into a set of *sub-goals* whose attainment will create the desired goal. Essentially, this means taking the problem, breaking it into the next biggest component problems, then breaking these in turn into smaller problems, and so on, until they reach manageable proportions. E.g. suppose one had the task of preparing a meal. This might be broken down into the sub-goals of getting food, consulting cookbooks, and finding a kitchen to cook it in. Each of the sub-goals could be broken into smaller problems (e.g. how to

get to the shops, what to purchase there, etc.). A problem with working backwards is that the sub-goals have often to be performed in a particular order, which may not at first be apparent (e.g. there is no point in going to the shops if one hasn't consulted the cookbook for the ingredients first).

working memory (WM) (1) A *short-term store* used to hold information temporarily whilst engaged in another task (e.g. in mental arithmetic, remembering the total of the columns added up so far whilst doing the rest of the sum). Also known as *general working memory (WMG)*. (2) The term is more commonly used to denote a specific model of working memory (*specific model of working memory (WMS)*), first posited by Baddeley and Hitch, and subsequently considerably modified. The model essentially consists of a central controller, called the *central executive*, which can itself hold in store a couple of items, but which usually passes on memorization tasks to specialized *slave systems*. These include a *phonological loop* (in early versions of the model, this was called the *articulatory loop*), which memorizes verbal materials (letters, words, and numbers); and a slave system for memorizing visual (what something looks like) and spatial (where items are located in space, or relative to each other) materials (the *visuo-spatial sketchpad*). The slave systems have a limited *capacity*.

working memory span (WMS) (1) Technique utilizing *working memory*, in which the subject is given a number of sentences to process (e.g. read out loud, judge whether meaningful etc.) with the instruction that s/he must try to remember the last word in each sentence seen. The span is a measure of the longest number of last words which can be accurately reported. (2) More generally, any *span* found in a *working memory task*.

writing output lexicon *Mental lexicon* which stores memories of how to produce written units.

WSE *word superiority effect.*

Y

Yerkes-Dodson law The phenomenon whereby, increasing the level of a subjects arousal at first improves his/her performance, until it peaks, and thereafter further arousal causes a decrease in performance. A graph of performance plotted against arousal level looks like an upside-down 'U' (hence, *inverted U curve*). The law does not hold for all situations, and the point at which the curve peaks varies between individuals and also depends upon the difficulty of the task.

Yngve depth An analytical technique which gives a 'score' for the *syntactic* complexity of a sentence or phrase.

Z

zeitgeist Spirit of the age – a set of views and values which characterize a particular school of thought in a particular historical epoch.

β **(beta)** See *signal detection analysis.*